UNBOXED

Conversations with My Ancestors

UNBOXED

Conversations with My Ancestors

Mary Ann Greenelsh

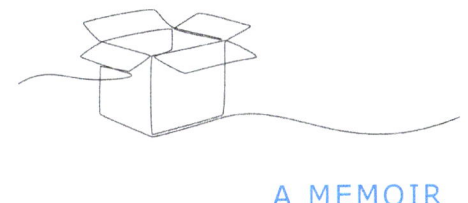

A MEMOIR

Edited by Martha Fuller
Layout and design by Sharon E Rawlins

SYNCHRONICITY PRESS
synchronicitypress24@gmail.com

ISBN 979-8-218-43839-5 Print
ISBN 979-8-218-43840-1 eBook

Printed in the United States of America

For my family—the past, present and future

CONTENTS

Preface

Taking a Leap and Diving In
Tea Leaves

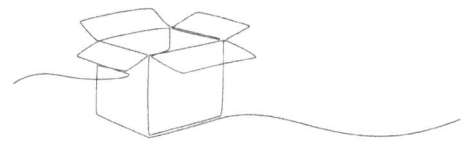

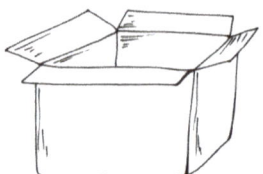

Taking a Leap and Diving In

Ancestors

One day during my teens, grandma handed me a box. "One day these will be valuable," she said. "Take care of them." The box contained some old Roseville pottery vases and a few pieces of costume jewelry — all I thought ugly at the time. So, I stashed it away. But over the years, I began to acquire family photos, artifacts, and other memorabilia. As I got older and relatives passed on, I realized someone needed to take care of the family memories and I felt that calling. Those memories, stored in multiple boxes, accompanied me from home to home and even comforted me from one life chapter to the next, like a cherished security blanket.

I had hoped to explore these ancestral memories with my dad in his retirement, as he too had always been interested in family history. Little research had been done on his mother's side of the family, the Rasgorsheks. Sadly, he died too soon. I feel his loss and curiosity, and miss his help navigating the unknowns and sharing his recollections of stories passed down. I think he would have loved being a part of the process.

When I contemplated my retirement and finally took the leap, I didn't really have a plan, but knew I wanted to reacquaint myself with my creative side. That part of me had been clamped down for years.

As I sat at my desk, I'd see the family boxes in my office closet peeking out at me. They began to speak louder and louder until I knew it was time to start digging. I got focused with writing, doing some art, and along with my husband, started diving into our respective family histories.

Soon after, I met Martha Fuller, my creative writing teacher, through the Otis College of Art and Design Extension program.

I am grateful for her expertise and inspiration, and her understanding of my crazy idea to tell my family stories in pieces like a puzzle.

At first, I did well just to come up with a few stories, but the ideas grew as the unboxing began. One of my challenges was how to weave them all together until I realized it had to be through my voice and reluctantly a few of my own stories. Except for "Oil and Water", the stories are about family members who are deceased. But I also have a glorious group of living relatives who make up the rest of my rich family fabric.

In the end, I chose to write where the boxes led me. And the stories evolved. Perhaps one day, there will be more stories to tell.

Tea Leaves

Quietly the Tea Leaves Are Speaking

Listening to My Ancestors

Genesis

Each of a Tree
Branches of the Tree
Hike of a Lifetime
Ancestors in Black and White
Boxes Calling

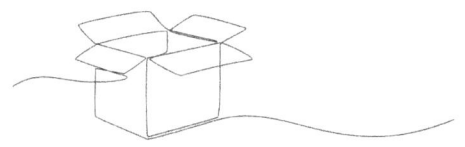

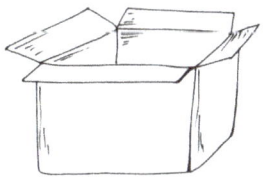

Each of a Tree

Each of a Tree

We are the deep roots of the past,
Birth lines and buried mysteries.
A cultivated culture of family lore.

With blazed trails and branches wide,
Our futures blend DNA, hope, and history.

We prune our complicated canopy,
Rich as we choose and wise as we wish.
New buds inspire fruitful growth.

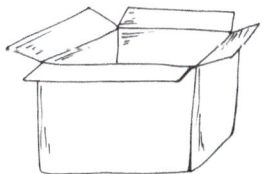

Branches of The Tree

W e are each like a tree — the one that grows in the yard, or forest, green with leaves, or needles. Comprised of branches and limbs reaching for the sun, we are grounded at our base with deep roots, circled by our rings of age and telling bark. Our roots, our foundation, hold us strong, as we seek the nourishing light. Our branches hold our lineage, stories, and DNA. Leaves reveal the details, personalities, siblings, parents, marriages, births, and deaths. Families and their foliage have seasons, get trimmed or grafted and some die off. It's nature and natural, and beautiful — the diversity that populates our lives, each its own and connected to the whole.

Four branches make up our basic tree, keys to our personal and varied heritage. I am a Greenelsh, Rasgorshek, O'Neil, York tree, as my brother would be — two branches from each of our parents' birth lines. These four lines are what connects the roots and that canopy of our biological family, our family brand. New seeds, or eventual withering, leave traces of our tree placement in the forest.

As the self-imposed, designated memory keeper, I am always curious, attached to preserving our family stories. I have a need to stay connected with our inherited cast of characters — those I cherish, those I miss, ones I never met, and the rest of us left to carry the torch of history, our roots, and all the connected fractures.

Everything in this world blooms, grows, and returns to its roots.
— Lao Tzu

Me Tending Family Headstones

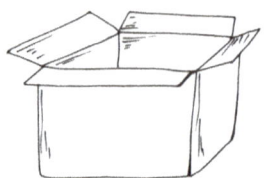

Hike of a Lifetime
2020

Me – Breathe, Release, Breathe On

A trip of a lifetime, a retirement gift, a spiritual journey, a personal pilgrimage — a turning point. My trip to the ancient Kingdom of Bhutan nestled between Tibet, India, and China — my Himalayan adventure.

After temple and monastery visits, a festival, cultural connections, exquisite scenery, and high elevation acclimation — the last day, Tiger's Nest. The infamous hike to a monastery on the side of a cliff, over 10,000 feet above sea level, established in 1692, is a pilgrimage for Bhutanese and worldly spiritual seekers. This part of the trip scares me.

The right shoes, snacks, water, sunscreen, a hat, and more water. Prayed up and practiced mantra, I'm ready to go — two miles up, two miles down, 700 stairs, 1700 ft. elevation gain. An endurance test for the body, mind. and soul. A spiritual quest. Not sure what to expect or why I even think this a good idea.

Our group arrives at the trail head — the pilgrimage welcome mat, a well-defined earthen carpet surrounded by tree draped mountains and evergreen scented aromas. No donkey rides up halfway or walking sticks, with few tourists — signs of early Covid 19 concerns, not yet felt at home. So far, so good. I can do this.

Ah, getting out in nature for a hike. A well-maintained trail — manageable. Breathing — still good. Social chat. The trail ahead visible — straight up. I start to feel it. Chat slows down. We all spread out. The work and inner journey supposed to begin. Time for the mantra — the inner chant. Repeat. Quietly repeat.

Om Ah Hung Vajra Guru Pemi Siddhi Hung

Or something like that.

After every switchback. Repeat. Stop, catch a breath, take in the moment, the aroma, the beauty. An older woman passes on her way down, I think German. Hellos and encouragement. Keep going.

Om Ah Hung Vajra Guru Pemi Siddhi Hung

Pronunciation sucks, stick with it.

I meet up with Jeff, a fellow journey mate, a new friend. We check in with each other and share our stories, his husband further up the trail, mine at home. We're both cancer survivors, knowing this hike, like treatment, a temporary struggle. Difficult, but doable. Life giving and our bodies know it. We stop and breathe — take it all in.

I continue.

Om Ah Hung Vajra Guru Pemi Siddhi Hung!

Almost to the top.

Om Ah Hung Vajra Guru Pemi Siddhi Hung!

The peaceful homeless dogs await, the prayer wheel and cafeteria at the halfway point. A place to refuel, have tea, a cracker, or a backpack granola bar. A place to pee. Tiger's Nest is now in sight! I'm workout tired and energized. A decision point — stop here or carry on.

Max, Jeff, Toni, Marcie, Lynn, me, and our guide Tshering — we choose to carry on. All determined, for different reasons. For me, I just must. Why? I don't know. Max has endless enthusiasm, Marcie a backpack full of snacks, and Toni a hike-saving aromatherapy oil in a little brown bottle called Breathe.

We consume the precarious spiritual vision of the famous Tiger's Nest and its addictive aura, take a few Facebook-worthy photos and preparatory inhales of Toni's Breathe oil. Now the stairs and a cliff edge-hugging well-traveled trail—a good guard-rail, but straight down—don't look. Jeff, paralyzed with his fear of heights, heads back. I empathize, send a prayer his way, but don't understand why I'm not also heading for the emergency exit—my master, fear, could hijack desire and mission. Don't go there. Carry on! Mantra forward.

More hikers now, mostly Bhutanese or Indian, take pictures, embracing their journey, a moment, our shared universal awe of Tiger's Nest. A waterfall to the left graces the massive rock wall the trail hugs. A collection of small stupas tucked in the rocks with prayer flags above, like little banners, wave heavenly messages, and frame the elusive goal in sight. One more set of steep stairs—we each drag in, one-by-one, to meet up with Tshering's warm smile and wealth of information.

First stop, bathroom. Always prepared, Tshering hands out strips of toilet paper for the drop and squat. Toni and I laugh as we try to remember the Sanskrit name of the yoga pose this resembles—and not think about our butts hanging off the side of a cliff. Malasana! Second stop, stash backpacks and shoes.

The monastery has several small sacred temple rooms to explore. A time to reflect and respect—no photos, only chanting hums, purposeful moments. Tshering who knows or is related to anyone important in Bhutan, locates the Lama, His Holiness. We meet him via a meditation he offers. I give my bracelets for his blessing, others give prayer flags, a scarf, pictures.

Silently. *Om Ah Hung Vajra Guru Pemi Siddhi Hung.*

We bow. I wonder if this is it, when I understand the deeper meaning of why I made this trek.

Tshering pulls us over to convey the Lama's special invitation. A whispered excitement as he ushers us to a secluded room. We're invited to have a latte before we leave. A latte with the Lama! Who knew?

Shiny silk fabrics cover three sofas surrounding a heater for an immediate five-cold-hiker-huddle on the floor, around the only warm spot in the place. A treasured latte machine stands on an unadorned table in the corner, a donated gift to the monastery, we learn. His Holiness serves up a hot cup of java—not the time to decline or inform of my distaste for coffee. Next to the latte machine sits a bowl of packaged Oreo cookies, as if purchased from a local Costco. A surreal moment—cliffside lattes and Oreo cookies with the Lama. There's meaning here—or at least a memory of a lifetime.

We fly back down on a caffeine rush and modest pride of accomplishment. A few tough stairs back; my legs are gone, hot soup at the cafeteria stop welcome. Whizzing down the switchbacks, no mantra, no more work or wondering—or fear. High fives from the rest of the group who stayed behind. This exhilaration, this joy means something. It starts to rain.

I don't know if a new truth or revelation will drop into my consciousness one ordinary day, or if it will remain just a well-kept, well-earned memory, well-worn over time. A reminder: I can face my fears, and whatever the next chapter in life brings.

One step at a time
I surrender to it all.
Breathe, release, breathe on.

Ancestors
In Black and White

Stare. It is the way to educate your eye, and more. Stare, pry, listen,
eavesdrop. Die knowing something. You are not here long.

— Walker Evans

Their world, as I know it, only exists in old black and white photos, in posed dour portraits and motionless family gatherings or travels. Still quiet lives. In my world, they live in a collection of snapshots and vast spaces of unknown, between whatever came before and after, a captured moment in time.

If only, a tiny wink, a faint hello from the grey photo haze frozen in their 3 x 5, or 5 x 7 framed existence.

If only, a warm embrace, to feel bone structure and smell a good, perfumed life, or of liquored toil, sweat and struggle — the aromas of life back then vs. their dust of now.

If only a thank you from their colorless voices. An invitation to share a cup of tea. To hear, "We're so happy to finally meet you".

If only I could find their footprints and follow their shadows to the place of my intrigue and imagination.

If only I could travel to a time when they live in multi-color — and my knowing is black and white.

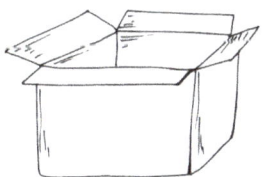

Boxes Calling

Me Amidst the Boxes

The trip and hike introduced me to the concept in Buddhism of the Beginner's Mind. My journey in this new life chapter was beginning and I could challenge myself, as in the hike. I could hear an inner voice propelling me forward. The boxes were calling!

I wonder if I'm the only one who finds boxes interesting. There's something comfortable in the contained and predictable four evenly connected walls. Sometimes covered, decorated, or wrapped, containing gifts, precious or everyday contents – even the box itself holds a function or memories – even secrets from the past.

My family repurposed almost every box. On a shelf in the hall closet, above where jackets and coats hung, and the vacuum cleaner and American flag were stored on the ready for service. Old See's candy, shoe, or perfume boxes, mixed with partially worn and torn gift boxes from various birthdays and holidays, on the ready for storage, gift wrapping, or school projects – a good box was always kept.

Mom kept her closely held memories and secrets in such a box – a pre-decorated Christmas one, for a shirt or blouse and a little flimsy, with numerous rubber bands securing it. I knew where it was, in her mystery stash of stuff, stored inside another box, in the back of her closet. It was private and stayed that way until her death, when I quickly took possession of it to protect from inquiring minds, other than my own.

Boxes hold treasures and tales – and I inherited the need to save and connect with them. I started to hear little rumblings from boxes in the closet in my new project office-yoga-guest room. "Come get us out of here. Our stories have been waiting for you. Please don't forget us."

The boxes awaited, and I had no more excuses. So, the excavation and raising of the dead begins.

A Box Awaits

Ordinary Family

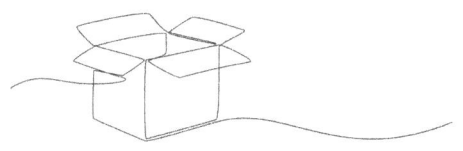

1970
Prom
Glamour Shots
Mom's Missing Decade
Patchouli Oil
Mom's Notebook
The Perfume Box
Mom's Plan
In Focus
The Pipe Tobacco Can
Uncomfortable
The Last Photo
A Day of Rest
Dad—The Good Boy
Cheating, Maybe
The Last Time I Saw Danny
Missing Danny
Oil and Water

1970

Me, Dad, David, Mom, Danny

Wewere an ordinary family, two parents, three kids, and a blue Chevy Impala, or maybe the white Ford Fairlane, or the beige Pontiac Bonneville. Always a new used car.

1970—me trying to figure out pre-teen fashion (yes, bobby socks and white sandals!) next to Dad in his already irritated dad position. In the middle, David after a few scoldings no doubt, and Mom stylish in her safe navy-blue funeral, wedding, graduation dress. Danny towers over us all while his motorcycle and the family dog, Pepper, await at home.

We were very white, but not ordinary. Maybe beige.

1972 Dad left. This was my mom's fourth marriage—she was 14 years older. I don't know when Danny started drinking.

Another Day — Summer 1964

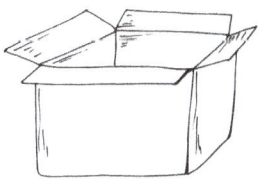

Prom

Prom Night 1977

Prom pictures are loaded. With dated fashion, memories, good, bad or cringe-worthy, it's one of those photos that got framed, sat on proud parents' mantles or shelves, and later saved in boxes and closets. We keep them—and occasionally go to remember.

I didn't love or hate high school. I wasn't popular, or unpopular. While capable of more, I settled into mediocrity. Starting with a good dose of insecurity, pimples, and braces, I embraced average, wanting to fit in but not stand out. I was one of few kids in a small town with divorced parents. A single mom working hard at the local K-Mart and a caring dad getting on with his new life.

I could take or leave prom. I didn't want to miss out but didn't yearn for the big event. My group of friends made plans to go, and we all had or found dates. Tom, my girlfriend's brother was mine—sweet and a little shy, like me. Plans and dates were in order but meaningless without the infamous attire.

My group of friends were good kids, smart, somewhat worldly interested, and artistically minded. A 1970s surfer vibe, reggae, weaving peer group with a few pukka shells. We vintaged shopped before it was cool, which is where I happened to find a new long dress, tags still intact, for $1.99. It was quite nice, I thought, and might even work for the prom. The price matched my enthusiasm.

I mentioned the prom to dad and told him about my great dress find. He was horrified, not at the dress, but with the idea that his daughter had to purchase her once-in-a-life-time prom dress at the local Goodwill. Out came the checkbook and demand that my stepmom take me to get a proper dad-approved dress. We found a lovely special event-worthy, white lacy number and matching uncomfortable white vinyl shoes. Dad felt better.

After obligatory corsage and boutonniere exchange and a snapshot in front of the fireplace, we were off to dinner, a pre-prom party and then the big auditorium-decorated event. For me, a blur, due to the partying part of the pre-party. I remember arriving at the prom and puking in the parking lot—probably more than once. My sweet and more in control date had no choice but to take me home. He saw that I was fine as I slung into the sofa amongst freshly folded laundry in the dark living room, where prom photos were taken hours earlier. My mom and brother had already gone to bed. Tom wisely left.

The next morning's pink stains on the lovely white lacy prom dress, illustrated a messy night was had. I felt horrible and had obviously been up to more than I should have. Mom brought a cup of tea and sat next to me on my bed. She wasn't mad, but a little concerned. Recognizing a teachable and tender moment, she shared a similar story she experienced with my dad when they were married. A business-related event took them to La Quinta in Palm Springs in the 1960s, when La Quinta was an exclusive resort. She still swooned telling the story of Cary Grant kissing her hand at the swanky affair. No doubt fancy free drinks were flying, and she imbibed a bit too much. Dad was embarrassed. She went on to council me and gently made it clear that I would not be calling in sick to work. Meanwhile, my brother David ironed my skirt.

I don't have fond or many memories of my prom. But I cherish those around it related to family and friends. High school was just four average years, from a collection of highs and lows. The photo reminds me of a memorable event worthy of a $1.99 dress and the warmth of those who cared about me.

Me with Friends

Glamour Shots

Mom

These two photos of Mom are my personal favorites, what I call her glamour shots. Likely taken in the 1940s, her missing decade years, when she took off from her rural roots in central California for presumably a larger, perhaps wilder life in numerous other states. Her ticket to leave was an early marriage in 1941 at 19, to her first husband in Las Vegas, followed by a second marriage in 1944 in Georgia. Then a one month stay at the Mayo Clinic in Minnesota, where she was abandoned by husband number two. At 29, she made her way back home to California saddled with medical bills — and a lot of life experience.

I take apart and turnover frames around her pictures in hope of clues. The reflective pose at the muted color fountain is part of a larger photo folded so it could fit into a white and gold trimmed wood frame. Two green thumb tacks secure a piece of string on the back for hanging on a wall. For whom? Herself? A husband or lover? Or something she sent home to her mother to suggest she was thriving in her new life. Perhaps also hinting of dueling truths — thriving for the camera, and her other self, maybe holding back secrets.

The black and white more classic portrait is small, something that could fit into a wallet, frame and photo as one unit, generated out of a Photomatic arcade machine, as per the notations on the back. Both photos suggest happy, romantic times.

The idea of moms and glamour don't go together, at least in my family. But, like us daughters and granddaughters, they were young and flirty at one time. Their domestic tags, rural or small-town roots, and the passing of time hid any nature of once embraced wild desires.

But they also lived with a lot of rules and condemnation for breaking them, and Mom broke her share. Her missing decade was a well guarded era in her life she didn't disclose, though she occasionally dropped mysterious random snippets of life once lived in Michigan, South Dakota, or Florida.

And so, my probing investigation carries on. There were dark times and marriages I know little about. But I'd like to think she had some damn good times too. I hope these glamour shots reveal just that.

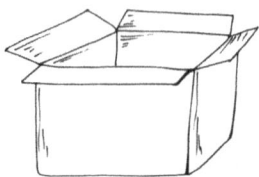

Mom's Missing Decade

Mom

O n Christmas Eve, coincidentally what would have been my mother's 101st birthday, my cousin Neil and I had breakfast at an old favorite café my mom and her sister used to visit in Paso Robles, CA. Now, a quiet place, Neil shared a story of my mother told to him by his grandmother.

"She left at gunpoint!" he said.

I also learned another clue that day about my mother's missing decade that made me question what I thought was a solid timeline in my investigation. Apparently, Mom had come back to California briefly during her decade away. At least that's how this story goes—filled with facts, suppositions, and a few curveballs.

Mom never talked about the period of her life after her childhood and before suburban life with my dad (her 4th husband), children, afternoon soap operas, and getting dinner on the table at 6 pm. She deflected the subject of her previous life, though she'd drop a random memory here and there about food, or some other unimportant but significant tidbit. Over a piece of Key Lime pie, she'd mention how much she liked it when she lived in Florida. Or the fact that she had also lived in Michigan and South Dakota. On the surface these were interesting, albeit puzzling bits and pieces of her past life, but underneath she was hiding darker parts of a previous decade—early 1940s to early 1950s.

My mom, Doris Kathleen O'Neil, born Dec. 24, 1921. She was the last of four children from parents who had a homestead in rural central coastal California, near her grandfather's winery in Templeton where her mom Lulu was raised. Her dad Timothy, an Irish immigrant also settled there to grow cherries and grapes for York Mountain winery. As the youngest, a surprise late baby in the O'Neil clan, she felt a like an outsider in age and with her interests. Mom was an artistic rebel at heart. A naive and restless dreamer.

As I pry through her private papers she left buried in a box in her closet, I flash back to that pensive look on her face when we almost ventured into the forbidden subject. Am I doing the right thing uncovering these hard cast stones? Out of respect and fear of stepping into the deep end, I held back when she was alive, but I always thought there was a part of her that wanted to say her piece and let go of a heavy burden. So, I dive in.

In a 1940 Census, my mom is listed as 18 years old, living at home with her mother in Paso Robles, CA. She graduated

Box with Diary and Letters

Templeton High School in 1939 and after attended the Santa Barbara School of Cosmetology. Dances were popular and one of the few forms of entertainment in those days. Camp Roberts, a nearby army base brought young men to the Paso Robles area during the war years, and Mom was no doubt "looking" and looking pretty with her friends. In a diary I found, tied tightly with numerous pieces of string, her writings reflected a bored and boy crazy teenager, perhaps with secrets left to what was not said between the lines.

Mom's Diary

Mom and Roland

On April 25, 1941, at just 19, Mom married Roland W. Voltz in Las Vegas, NV. He was from California but possibly had family connections in Michigan. Mom probably met him in Paso Robles, perhaps through friends or at a dance, or two, and fell for a new adventure. It was rumored that he may have been dodging the draft, therefore skipping town with a lovestruck young woman, eleven years younger than him. I don't know if Mom knew of his previous marriage that ended in divorce, (due to cruelty), or that her marriage would share the same fate several years later. These had to have been exciting but scary times for her.

Mom and Roland

Roland

Mom and Bill

On May 29, 1944, at the age of 22, Mom married William (Bill) F. Gibbs. I don't know how or where Mom connected with Bill Gibbs, or the details on how or where she left Roland. Both Bill and Roland were born in 1910, and worked in the automobile business — auto body, mechanics type work. I wonder if they knew each other and if Mom met them through some common thread in California, Michigan, or somewhere else. Was she in a desperate place having left Roland, or was she hiding from him? How did she facilitate that? What stories did she have to alter to get out of a bad place?

Bill was also a divorcee, and photos suggest a loving father. He had connections and lived in South Dakota. In Mom's stash

This is Bill and I taken
this same day. You had
better take a good look at
him because I'm going to
marry that man and as
Louise said "you can't
marry just Daddy, you
have to marry us", We
have such fun together
    Some day when you
meet him, you will
be proud to know
such a man as he
is. I think he is
wonderful

Mom and Bill

Bill

of memorabilia was an old napkin from the Pierre Municipal Bar and Lounge—no doubt a cherished moment. But they got married in Macon, Georgia, where Bill's sister resided—the same place Bill filed a petition for divorce from Mom in 1949.

Mom mentioned that Bill was a traveling salesman, which if true, may make it understandable as to why Mom lived with his family in Florida for an extended period, seemingly without him much of the time. She became close to all of them, including his children and kept letters and old Christmas cards from lifelong correspondence.

1946–1947, Family Gathering in California

This photo is during the heart of Mom's missing decade, according to Neil's timeline. My mom third from the right, amongst her mother, siblings, and their families—my cousin Neil, second child from the left. The man next to my mom was referenced with the photo as Steve, her husband. Though, I think it's Bill—I have no idea how or where a Steve fits into her history. And I don't know why they are in California. Mom's body language suggests she is in a very uncomfortable situation. If only her limbs could talk—and maybe, they are.

Mom and BIll

1945, September 24 — Mom filed a petition for divorce from Roland Voltz, in Wayne, Michigan, reason, Cruelty, no children. It was granted. 1946, January 16 — divorce was final.

1949, June/July — Bill filed a petition for divorce in Macon, GA.

1949 — Mom was residing in Seminole, FL (Bill Gibbs' family lived in Sanford, FL)

1949, Late October. Mom was at the Mayo clinic for tests. She had numbness and pain in her limbs and back, fearing Multiple Sclerosis (MS). November 5, she had surgery to have a tumor removed from her spine. Thankfully, it wasn't MS. She's there for a month recovering. Letters home to her mom and sister reflected the mom we knew, always seeing the best in her situations and describing all the details around her five ailing roommates and passable food. She mentioned Bill coming to visit but that he would have to return to South Dakota — and for them not to worry. Mom was open to us about the fact she had back surgery and spent a month at the Mayo Clinic. Perhaps unavoidable due to the long vertical scar from her neck to waist. Later she dropped the comment that Bill had also abandoned her there.

1950 Census — Rapid City, SD. Mom was 28 and the wife of William Gibbs. Also living in the home was Nellie, Bill's youngest child from his first marriage.

1950, October — San Luis Obispo, CA. Mom, Doris Gibbs, began receiving firm but kind letters from the Mayo Clinic concerning her bill for $560. They could not find the $80 payment she claimed Bill had made. They offered an adjustment to $194.65. She began making payments of $10/month.

1950, October — Bill Gibbs petitioned State of CA for annulment of his marriage to Kathleen Gibbs, also known as Doris Gibbs. He claimed that she was not divorced at the time of his marriage to her in 1944. Mom had used her middle and maiden name (Kathleen O'Neil), suggesting that she (and probably Bill too) knew she was still married to Roland at the time.

There are many gaps in Mom's missing decade and still much to be learned. Snippets I vaguely remember hearing, I still can't place.

She claimed she broke her jaw during this period when she fell at a wedding. She would show us her crooked bite. I assume this was related to the cruelty of Roland, or was it, Bill? or a Steve? She also mentioned involvement in a serious auto accident somewhere. I wonder if the tumor that grew in her spine, and lasting scar was a reminder of her big adventure, with a couple of fractured men.

What else did Mom keep close in her guarded core? More shameful stories in the dark side of being with these older men who amused and abused her? What parts did she play in the sagas? How many tears, how much heartbreak, how many lonely times? And how much of her hope and naivety paved the way forward, backward, and forward again until she made it home.

Both Roland and Bill's lives continued to unravel, with marriages, alcohol, and the law. My brother David vaguely remembered Mom mention a Steve who lived in Lompoc, also on the central coast in California. In 1943, a Steve Voltz was named in a new Shell Gas Station advertisement. Did Roland possibly go by the nickname Steve or use it when he needed to avoid his legal name? In 1947, Roland was accused of attempted murder with his newly divorced 3rd wife, attempting to drive her off a cliff. Bill was arrested and posted bail in a Montana jail for petty larceny in 1954. Mom returned to her roots on the California central coast, where she began working at the Poultry Department at Cal Poly San Luis Obispo. She no longer sought out older bad boys, but she was still a bit naïve and boy crazy, this time cute college students—a beginning theme for her next decade.

During her last day in hospice, after being with her for several weeks in September 2016, I pondered what more I needed to say at her bedside, so she could be released from her 94 years. The only thing left— her missing decade, always shrouded under a heavy cloud. I held her hand and told her that whatever it was she was afraid to share, that it was okay. We benefited from the mom she became, and we were proud of her. She could let it go—and she did.

Mom

Patchouli Oil

My mother was the first feminist I knew. Not a flag waving, or bra burning one, but a hardworking single mom. A single mom in a small town of seemingly perfect and happy intact families, at least to me.

Standing up for change wasn't Mom's reason for going it alone. Mom and Dad likely grew apart, with their age difference and Dad's career in transition as contributing factors. But Dad the younger, was older in his ideas on his wife's role. Mom having a job and meaning (and perhaps means), was not a secure place for him. Everyone had a lane. For him, the freedom seeking 60s were just a distraction. Feminism a foreign and uncomfortable concept. I believe family was both their committed place, but change was brewing.

Enamored with the hippies and their movement, Mom was drawn to the message of freedom, peace, and resistance of conformist ideas. It tapped into the part of her repressed past I never knew, her unfulfilled artistic talents and growing metaphysical interests. Did she have rebellious rumblings speaking to her when she ironed Dad's shirts, bed sheets and tablecloths as she watched her soap operas every afternoon from 2:30–3:30? I only knew the joy of getting to iron his handkerchiefs and pillowcases, after school — easy perfect simple squares.

Strong women run in my family, whether quiet and conforming, or a little rebellious. My mom was both. A traditional, but single mom with an adventurous yet reserved nature, she couldn't deny either.

One Christmas, my aunt Gloria gave Mom some Patchouli oil. Gloria was married to Uncle Norm and lived in LA, was educated, stylish and at the center of any good time. Gloria added the oil to a more traditional holiday gift, like a little inside secret. It intrigued us all — magenta tissue wrapped around a mysterious small brown bottle. The pungent aroma made an exotic, free loving statement, perhaps more than desired, but Mom now had a real piece of hippie life, even if it only sat on her vanity.

But what wasn't ok to me, was an incident with Play-girl magazine. Feminism turned the tables on Playboy and Mom somehow got a copy and hung the male centerfold picture in her bathroom. We all used the shower in her bath-room, so it wasn't a private space for displaying anything suggestive. I was 14 when I spotted the total dereliction of Mom's duties! Horrified, I ripped it down, marched down the hallway and confronted her. I had to be the mature adult to keep what was left of this family intact and safe, and I gave her a piece of my incensed mind! She laughed, thought it was funny. Clearly, I did not.

Her rebellious escapist moment was killed by her moral-authority, torch-carrying daughter, and reminded of her place at the head of the kitchen table. Her free and fantasy filled years well behind her. She was responsible, loved her kids more than anything and knew her lane as a single mom in a small town—but maybe the only mom with Patchouli oil.

Mom's Notebook

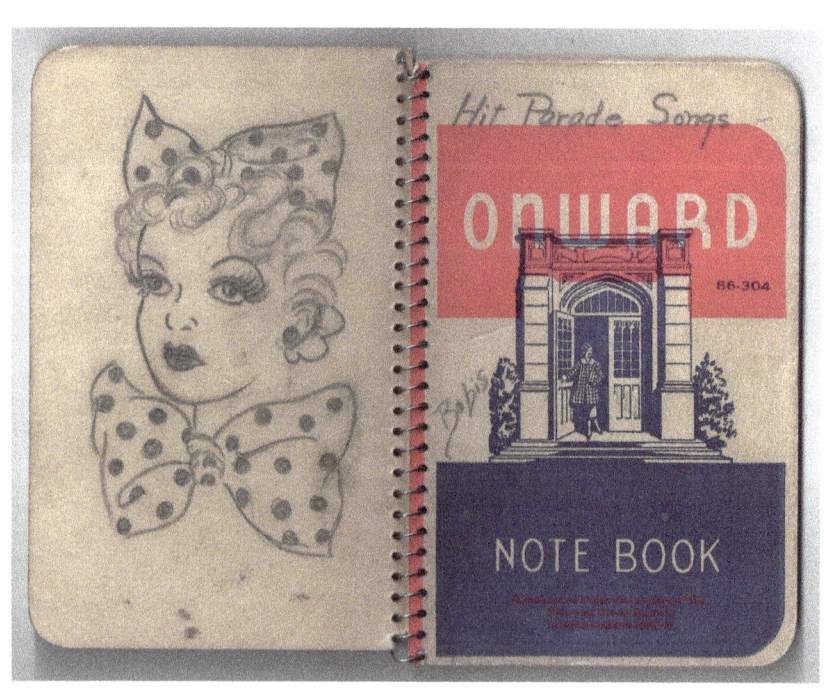

Mom's Notebook

I don't know if it was a unique hobby or something teenagers did in the 1930s. But Mom and her friends wrote down lyrics to songs they would hear on the radio. I have several little notebooks in Mom's familiar handwriting organized with lyrics from songs like "While a Cigarette was Burning" or "Who Blew Out the Flame" or one of her favorite Cole Porter songs, "Begin the Beguine". When she had all the lyrics completed, she wrote done on the top and the date. These were in 1938-39, her high school years. On the back of a small notebook of lyrics is one of her random sketches.

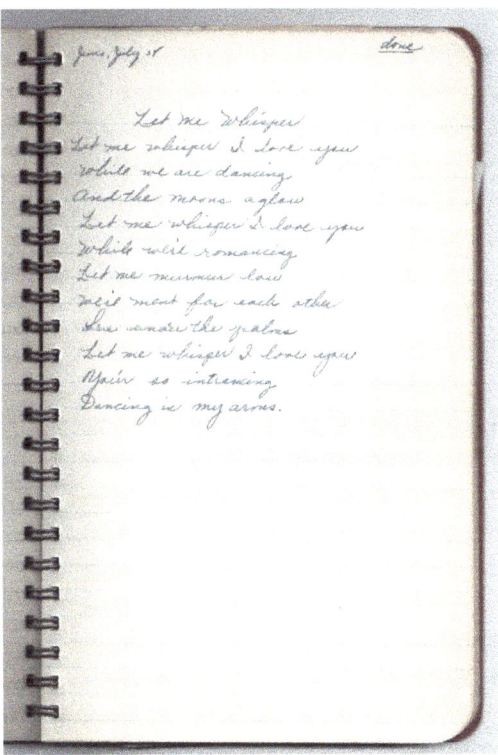

Popular Song Lyrics Mom Memorized
and Wrote in Her Notebook

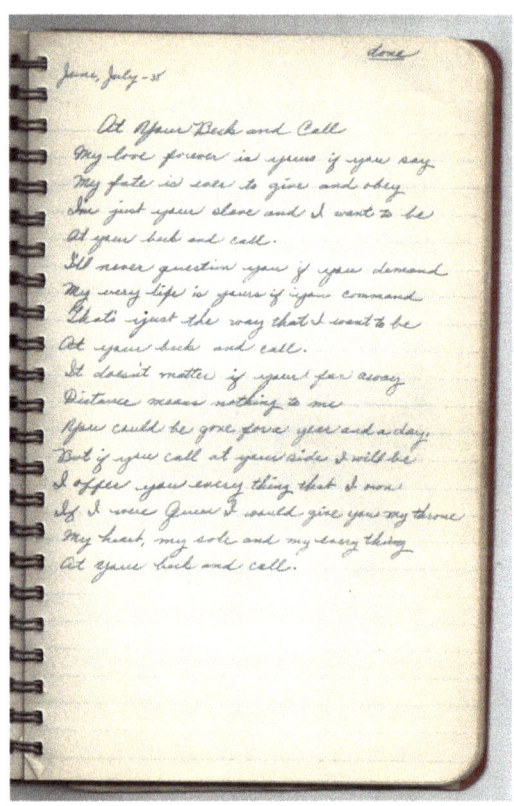

Popular Song Lyrics Mom Memorized
and Wrote in Her Notebook

Popular Song Lyrics Mom Memorized and Wrote in Her Notebook
One of Mom's Sketches

Mom's Sketches

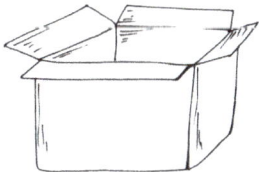

The Perfume Box

The Old Perfume Box

I come across an old familiar perfume box in Mom's bin of memorabilia she kept along with old pictures and yearbooks. I remember the day Dad brought it home.

It was a typical early evening, Mom in the kitchen making dinner and us kids in the living room watching TV or playing a game, prior to Dad's arrival home.

Dad with a lighter step and disposition, looked like he had a good day when he walked in the door. He had a gift for Mom and presented her an elegant box. A little giddy and surprised to receive an unexpected gift on an ordinary day, she stopped what she was doing. We listened in.

From the kitchen came a loud squeak, followed by a squeal, and a laugh, then another laugh. Of course, we had to go see what was going on. The perfume box was a joke, a novelty gift—a beautiful perfume box on the outside, but when opened, out sprung a wretched looking gray rat. While Mom shared in the fun, I could see the subtle letdown. Dad was in stiches. Mom went back to cooking dinner. Dad had stories to take back to the office the next day.

The box remained parked on a bookshelf in the living room. And for years, we kids had fun offering a gift of perfume to visiting friends and relatives.

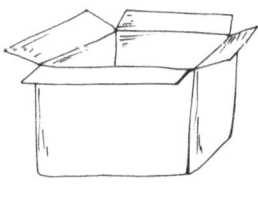

Disappointment and Faith

After a drive for lunch at the beach, inclusive of dessert, we drove past a popular ice cream shop.

From the backseat of the car, Mom excitedly asked, "Anyone want an ice cream?"

"No! I was quick to say. "We just had a big dessert."

Deflated, she sulked, "You're no fun."

It was not unusual for Mom to be quietly disappointed, when her ideas were met with imperfect reality. Parts of her life did not go as she had wanted. But she also set high expectations that holidays, vacations, or other family gatherings would be flawless— that everyone would rise to the occasion, be prepared, on time and share her vision of happy times. While there were many fine moments, there were plenty she had to accept as is.

Mom always hung on to memories and faith. When Dad was in a coma in the hospital after a massive stroke, many years past their divorce, my brother brought her in to say goodbye. My stepmother, siblings and I had all agreed and made the decision that Dad would not want potential life-saving surgery. The outlook for survival was grim, a vegetated state at best. Letting him go, while much too soon, was the unanimous sad decision. Mom always held out hope for miracles and secretly wished we could have tried. But she also knew it wasn't her place and a final goodbye to Dad and her memories was all that was left.

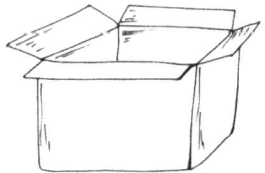

Mom's Plan

I t was somewhere in the early mid 1980s and Mom had a plan. She was excited about a speaker coming to her small church in her small town that she called home. Edwene Gaines, a rag to riches minister, who promoted spiritual prosperity thinking in her teachings, writings, and seminars. Respected on the bigger new age stage, she was making her way through Mom's town.

Mom requested and made it clear that she wanted her kids to join her at this church gig. It was important and fascinating. And we were expected.

I lived several hours drive away and made plans to go home that weekend for the Saturday afternoon workshop. I'm sure my brothers preferred doing something different, but we all showed up. Mom was happy, joined by her kids, sitting side-by-side on the wooden church pew to hear some spiritual truth.

Going to church was important to my mom in our early years. Perhaps something she didn't get enough of in her childhood. Or a desired protective foundation to keep her kids from a divorced home, from going astray — or repeating some of her past choices. In our teen years, church wasn't pushed on us, but a weekly Bible reading around the kitchen table was required. Just one passage. We got it. Can we go now?

Edwene was a bundle of southern belle charm, wit, and profound enthusiasm. She told her story and inspired godly spiritual prosperity thinking. I was into it and intrigued. My brothers paid attention. Mom sat with motherly satisfaction. We were compelled to get some religion, so to speak. But it was a workshop, not a one-way lecture.

We were handed paper and pencils and Edwene asked us to do some internal digging. Write down our thoughts and be willing to share them. I can't remember the specific assignment, but my brothers and I followed along, thinking, writing, looking inside. But Mom just sat there. She wasn't having anything to do with it. Not going there and not impressed, she sat in motherly judgement of Edwene's program.

Mom wanted that righteous nugget of truth to land into our collective laps. The Aha! The, I told you so. That solid gold metaphysical pearl of spiritual wisdom, channeled via Edwene, and infused into her offspring to help keep us safe, wise, and close to her, as we went about our lives. She didn't want to dig, or share an unprotected moment, a powwow with her kids. She just wanted us all together, guided by her motherly love, on a Saturday afternoon.

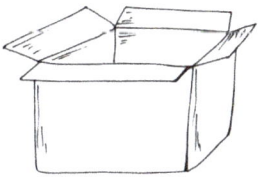

In Focus

Me, David, Mom, Danny

It's an average 1970s photo, now varnished in a cataract haze. But there are some photos that capture a pivotal moment of unbeknownst importance. This was one of those. A family snapshot taken a day or two prior to my oldest brother Danny's wedding. He was 21, getting married and leaving home for the first time. With my younger brother David leaning to my left, we casually posed for the camera. Mom and Danny seem to grasp the meaningful moment in a pensive stare, focusing on a shared connection point. A significant change was about to happen. The first born was leaving. Was Mom possibly scanning her past marriage journeys and the passage of time, as she embraced the inevitable with pride, love, and hope?

The Pipe Tobacco Can

The Pipe Tobacco Can

75

Mom liked the occasional aroma of pipe tobacco and cigar smoke. It was manly and evoked memories from various chapters of her past. The whiff would momentarily take her back to a place. But I remember the odor differently. Stale smoke imbedded in a relative's house, usually someone very old. Or being around said uncle with the stinky habit hanging out of the corner of his mouth. Dad smoked cigarettes. That was bad enough.

The vintage can in Mom's box has a hint of some smell, maybe old tobacco, but more like something that hasn't been opened in years. It contains sewing items, but it's mainly a collection of buttons. Cool old buttons. And empty spools of thread — not sure why she kept them. And an old, tarnished silver thimble. I wish I knew its story. Most every woman in the past owned a thimble for mending, darning, patchwork, and embroidery. It's too big for Mom. Her fingers were thin, like mine, and it doesn't fit me. But why is any of this saved with her other personal items from the past? The old can and its contents — stored away memories, I'll never know.

Uncomfortable

S he leaned on the stool at the end of the kitchen counter, trying to sit as if she was comfortable. It was Mom's last visit she made to our home before her final year. There in her travel robe, floral, pink with snaps down the front, and rosy slippers matching her swollen ankles, she sat pensive.

I wondered what she was thinking. Could it be the conversation she had with my husband Daniel the night before? She didn't understand much about the Internet, but she understood that he was an investigator. She was curious, as if she wanted to find something, but didn't want anyone else to.

I didn't ask.

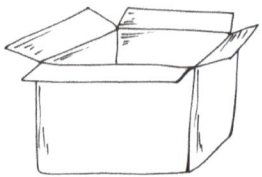

The Last Photo

Mom, Me, David

This is the last photo I have with my mother—my brother David is in the background. It was July 4, 2016.

After a neighborhood gathering and parade, we took this—just because. I knew it could be her last journey to my home. She was 94. Mobility and everyday activities were challenging, and she didn't think she could make the trip again. What I didn't know was that she was hiding a growing cancer—news she would share just weeks later. I wonder if that was on her mind in this moment. Our lives would be changing.

She died ten weeks later.

A Day of Rest

Blend of Spiritual Symbols

Religion wasn't a big part of my family culture. But attending church did occur for some and Sundays were an important day of the week—a day of rest for a few. Family Sunday dinners and gatherings assured little rest for women. Religious practice was left for those who kept their personal spiritual flame alive and maintained a sanctuary for family weddings and funerals.

Mom was raised in a home with mixed religions. Her mother's side, the York's, were Protestants, but not church goers. Her grandfather Andrew York was probably too busy to think about it, and his wife Huldah possibly left her traditions when she divorced her first husband, a fire and brimstone, meaner than a snake, preacher.

Mom's dad, Timothy O'Neil was a good Irish Catholic and she had fond memories of going to church with him in town. Coincidently, the local priest was also a good customer of the family wine making business.

Mixed religion mattered only in death—their souls rest in separate cemeteries.

My grandmother, on the Greenelsh side went to church and was a member of the Order of the Eastern Star. It gave her a social outlet and probably mattered to my grandfather that she, and he by association, were viewed as good Presbyterians. Grandpa held a stern judgmental torch that was likely passed down from his parents Fred and Winifred Greenelsh. Newspaper notices I found indicate they were active in their church and choir, but while aged, their hymnals and Bibles were pristine. The Rasgorsheks didn't seem to be regular church goers, but according to Aunt Gloria (raised in a non-religious Jewish family), a nervous-making

Jesus portrait hung on a guest bedroom wall. Uncle Norm remembered attending the "Little Brown Church" on Coldwater Canyon Ave. with his grandmother/mother Ethel Rasgorshek (where Ronald and Nancy Reagan were later married). Norm was irritated that the minister drove a fancy Cadillac, while he strongly asked for money for the church.

John Rasgorshek was active in the Masons. He became the High Priest in his local Masonic temple in Van Nuys, CA in 1936. His uncle, Gabe Rasgorshek, became interested in Christian Science when he came to LA. His book, *Science and Health, with Key to the Scriptures*, by Mary Baker Eddy is nestled in with the Bibles.

Mom saw to it that we went to church in our childhood years at a local American Baptist church — a more relaxed version of the denomination. Dad, like his dad, would drop us off and pick us up, but wouldn't step in. I think he liked his quiet couple of hours with everyone out of the house. That was his religion. But, when my parents divorced, Mom didn't feel accepted in a small-town church world where divorce wasn't common (and she had a few secretly stacked up). She always felt a spiritual connection, like her father did, but she was evolving.

On the day Mom died, we all thought about what she wanted and needed in her final hours. Family and friends had come and gone. My brother David, his daughter and I remained with the hospice workers. We gave her a lavender bath, opened the window and David read a Navajo poem. In the background I noticed that the TV was left on with *The Hollywood Medium* show playing. She would have liked that.

Dad–The Good Boy

Dad

I think of my dad when I look at old photographs, especially those from the Rasgorshek's, his mom's side of the family. He was interested in researching their family history, which had never been done before. I think he viewed it as a project for his retirement years, maybe something we could do together. Instead, I'm doing it alone, in my retirement years, perhaps a bit for him—a guiding light.

I never really got to know Dad's inner life and his reflections on his early years, and I don't know what family stories he heard while growing up. He was always a responsible man—organized, a little rigid, stern, and moody, but had a good sense of humor and a great smile I wish I had seen more, but his tense nature kept all fun in check. He stayed within the lines, like those he traced around tools on pegboard in the garage. His label maker assured all was filed in the right place.

Like his mother, Dad played the saxophone. I'd like to think he loved it. He toured with his college band, the Collegians. I found several newspaper articles and concert programs in Grandma and Grandpa's box. They were proud of him. Oddly, but perhaps expected, he was a Poultry major in college, carrying on the family business and perhaps becoming even more in their eyes. But Dad hated eggs and stiff jeans. He liked Duke Ellington and old cars. It wasn't surprising he didn't graduate and keep up with his music— he left a few months early, for reasons unlike that of a good boy.

Men's Glee Club

CALIFORNIA
STATE
POLYTECHNIC
COLLEGE

SIXTEENTH ANNUAL TOUR

H. P. DAVIDSON
DIRECTOR

Collegians

The Collegians Band

Marvin Greenelsh gets honor from Glee Club

Marvin Greenelsh, son of Mr. and Mrs. L. Paul Greenelsh of 23649 N. Pine Street, Newhall, has been selected to accompany the California State Polytechnic College's home campus glee club in the club's 1957 music tour.

Greenelsh, a poultry husbandry junior, is active in the music department. He is a saxophone player in the college band and in the Collegians, Cal Poly's widely known dance band. He will be one of 15 band members to accompany the glee club on its annual spring tour—one of the highest honors that can be paid to a Cal Poly musician.

Honor from Glee Club

Mom and Dad
1958

I like this photo. Mom looks as if she has a secret on her wedding day with my dad. And she did. To my dad, it was probably the reason for their marriage, June 7, 1958. I was born January 29,1959.

Mom finally settled down with a good man who would also adopt her 4-year-old son Danny from a previous marriage. Dad was young 22, Mom 36. Dad was just getting started, Mom had three marriages already — one divorce, two annulled.

They were brought together by the poultry profession. Mom worked examining eggs in the poultry department at Cal Poly San Luis Obispo. Dad was a poultry student. Perhaps college was his ticket out, choosing a parent approved major, in a parent approved town (where numerous Greenelsh's already lived). He was a musician and car enthusiast at heart, not an Aggie. He also worked in a music store— but soon he had to start thinking about supporting a family.

Mom liked her job in the poultry department. It was a place to begin building her life again after a decade away. She made friends, had a baby, and started to make it on her own. But her love was art. While her talent and interest never waned, it was always put on hold.

They found common ground and filled each other's needs, while on their respective life paths. Together, kids and home became their love. Their artistic desires became a domestic expression of mid-century suburban life. The saxophone got pulled out for my brothers' short-lived attempts at school band. Mom took an occasional art class. Dad made picture frames for her better pieces with his growing Dad woodworking skills.

Did their music die 14 years later when they grew apart? Perhaps their age difference played a role. Times were changing. Mom embraced being ok without a husband and lived the life of a single mom. Dad remarried and created a new second family.

They both just moved on.

We are all a product of those who raised us, for better or worse. Like Dad, my brother Danny and I followed the rules and lived within the lines. David, more like my mom, often followed his own path. Like them, we all divorced.

Dad died at 66, in 2003.
Mom died 13 years later at 94, in 2016.

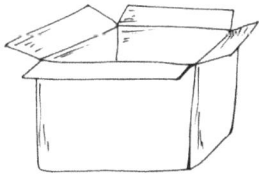

Cheating, Maybe

T he headline, *Cheating Scandal at Fishing Tournament Rocks Competitive Fishing World* reminds of two Dad stories. The online news story involved two pro anglers planting lead weights into their prized catch and winning thousands of dollars. A shocking scandal of intentional fraud. My dad's stories—an amateur angler, a competitive and caring dad, and a moment of opportunity—otherwise known as intentional cheating, maybe. He would have had a chuckle reading the news story, secretly admiring the balls and brilliance of their stupidity.

Dad was a hard worker, high-strung, easily stressed and stern. A salesman with the Gas Company, and then insurance, and a weekend home handyman of many projects. His creative palette—tan, light brown, straight lines, and right angles. But he enjoyed a good laugh, Lucky Strike cigarettes and Hamm's beer. Always busy keeping life in order—the outlines on the peg board in the garage surrounded every tool and labels were made with his label maker and affixed to the little drawers of nails and screws. There were rules to keep everything in order, and he followed them — most of the time.

Our well-organized summer family vacations, pulling a trailer on road trips of campgrounds, trout fishing, rock hounding and backseat sibling bickering — and endless miles exploring national parks, dinosaur exhibits or lava caves. It was on a trip to Oregon when Dad and my uncle Red got caught cheating — a mini family friendly scandal.

Legal with fishing licenses, and an eagerness to get a good catch, they found a sweet and fertile spot where the trout were plentiful. Their assumption that no one would know if they exceeded the catch limits came to a quick and stupid end. Upon a surprise visit from the fish warden, they swiftly threw back their overage into the still water. Their lies and the obvious floating evidence led to citations and a courthouse visit they could not ignore — followed by a family mea culpa.

In his well-organized garage, Dad got caught up in another amateur cheating moment. A dad and son project, the Cub Scout Pinewood Derby. In Dad's case more dad than son. An opportunity to create something — and to win. He loved model cars, projects and perfection and this was going to be a proud moment on the Cub Scout stage.

The finished product, a spectacular sporty, lacquered dark blue race car, with hand-painted sizzling red, orange and yellow flames. A sleek aerodynamic beauty, carved out of a pine box shape of wood. It radiated speed but wasn't heavy. There were strict rules about materials, size and weight for the gravity fueled race, but Dad had a solution—that maybe no one would notice. He melted down lead he used for making fishing weights and poured the liquid silver nugget into a hole he carved in the wood, underneath the flaming front end of the car. Problem solved. But the scheme didn't fare well on the day of the race. The car looked like a high-gloss and obvious winner, but upon inspection the lead weight was detected. My dad and brother had to accept disqualification or remove the rule breaking amendment. At least the car looked fabulous as it trailed behind in flaming glory!

There were other moments when Dad colored outside the lines. When my parents divorced, he bought a red sports car, grew a mustache, played tennis, and took an art class. For a moment, he was the guy that maybe he wanted to be if he had taken a different path. I wonder what his life, would have been like, had he followed his dreams as a musician. While he played saxophone in the college band, during the big band years, and worked in a music store, he was pursuing a degree in Poultry, that he never finished—or desired. Like his Duke Ellington, Bennie Goodman, and Peggy Lee albums he later kept stored in the hallway closet amongst the sheets and towels of domestic life, his unstructured creative expressions were tucked away in family responsibilities—and an occasional cheat, maybe.

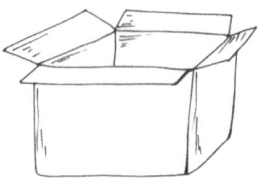

The Last Time I Saw Danny

March 2018

Danny – Christmas 2017

I relished my reluctant sneak out of the office lunch time visits to the rehabilitation center in Gardena, south of LA. Larry Flint's Lucky Lady Casino adjacent — the only location that would take Danny's insurance, take him to dialysis, and basically take him at all. Sadly, he fit in the drab facility, his last stop — a collection of forlorn or forgotten lives. He had already been kicked out of other rehab centers — belligerent encounters with nurses and refusal to do physical therapy, his usual game plan. The frayed grey drapes and shiny clean floors, like my brother's life, didn't make sense to me.

Somewhere between divorce and alcohol, his path and weakness led him to a reclusive and rural life, with his fears and secrets intact. His definition of living — off the grid, and always in control — except for the never mentioned alcohol. He acquired doctors, rehab stays, hospital visits, meds, and bills, while losing limbs and any quality of life. Happily deteriorating.

His good life brought him to a street view of Larry Flint's on Rosecrans. Our conversations were some of our best. He would look at me, looking at him — me assessing how many slabs of butter he slathered on his toast — as if it mattered. And with a sly grin he'd claim, "You gotta live".

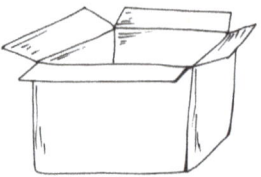

Missing Danny

Christmas 2018 — David, Karen, Me, Julia

D ad, like the Greenelshs and Rasgorsheks on his side of the ancestral tree, took many photos to document various gatherings and moments. He liked to assemble all his children for a picture, when he could—during the holidays, a special event, like a wedding, or maybe just a simple Santa Maria style summer BBQ in his backyard. This started as early as I can remember and carried on after Dad remarried and had two daughters, my half-sisters Julia and Karen. And, true to my dad's need for order and rituals, as he took the photo(s) we all stood in the same position each time. We continue the tradition today, when we can—and each time remember Danny—and of course, Dad too.

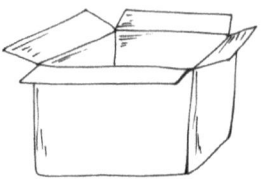

Oil and Water

Mom Holding David with Me at the Beach

I can't help but want to send my brother David one of my daily health focused emails with links to articles on healthy aging or understanding how to eat an anti-inflammatory diet — a natural urge for this big sister trying to show how right I am. That sisterly nudge. The replacement mom. The fearing and worrying nature in me that wants to assure that David sticks around in my life longer than Danny did. We are the last of our original family unit. Nearly alone.

David and I are both competitive and a bit bossy by nature — probably a trait we got from Dad — certainly not Mom. We bickered incessantly according to Mom's constant plea for us to stop. We knew to behave better around Dad. Perhaps normal for siblings born just 18 months apart and often referred to as a unit — Mary Ann and David. We were close, yet different.

David is smarter than me, a natural born teacher. Or in my case, sometimes a natural born irritant. He probably felt the same about me — a sensitive *do-gooder*. I got ahead by following the rules and my internal need to take care of others. David followed his independent streak and need to test the rules. I was the one who colored within the lines and made pretty little flowers. David was the one who scribbled and purposely caused a bit of havoc.

I couldn't help myself to over-decorate the dining room table when Dad was bringing home a peer from work for dinner. I attached little wire-stemmed flowers to as many utensils as possible, until Mom insisted I tone it down a bit. David couldn't help himself with a friend, to over decorate a neighbor's white sportscar. They found cans of spray paint in the trunk and proceeded to explore their artful ways on an expensive white canvas. Dad had to pay for the artwork.

But David and I were, and still are a team. A built-in collaborative unit when we need to be. Especially when it involves caring for our family, and each other.

Mom's birthday was Christmas Eve. She frequently had to work. A retail job assured of that. And with my siblings, we were tasked with numerous household chores. On one Christmas Eve, the water faucet broke when one of us (probably David) was washing up dishes. Hot water shot up to the kitchen ceiling and wouldn't stop until Danny could come to the rescue. Water dripped down through every cupboard and created huge puddles on the floor. Knowing Mom was working hard and on her birthday, David and I cleaned out every cupboard, re-lined each shelf with new shelf paper, re-washed every dish and surface. We were on a mission. Despite the stench of wet wood, Mom was proud of her kids and her super clean kitchen.

Now that Mom, Dad, and Danny are gone, David and I must work harder to stay connected. We do *The New York Times* Wordle game each morning now—a daily competition to see who is momentarily smarter, or luckier. David is having a bit of a bad streak this week. Or, I'm just having an exceptionally good streak. I start to look at my emails for an article on some subject about how to ward off Alzheimer's or build better brain cells. I can't help myself.

Mom's Side
Yorks and O'Neils

The Big Dog

Little Dog

Lulu

Irish Roots

The Black Letter

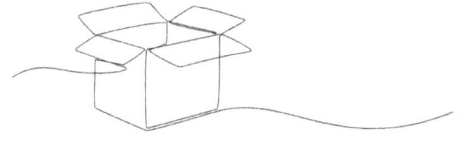

Mom's Side

YORKS & O'NEILS

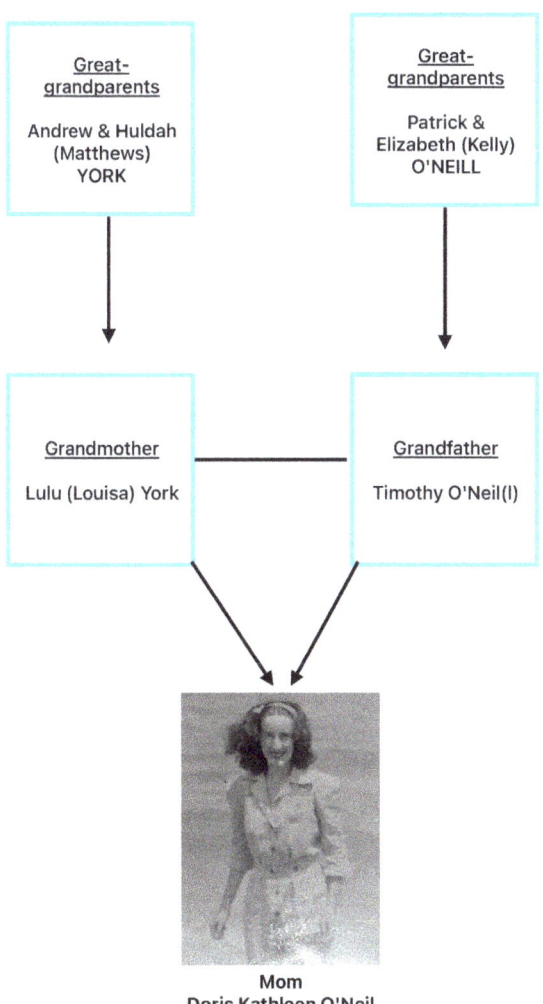

Great-grandparents	Great-grandparents
Andrew & Huldah (Matthews) YORK	Patrick & Elizabeth (Kelly) O'NEILL

Grandmother	Grandfather
Lulu (Louisa) York	Timothy O'Neil(l)

Mom
Doris Kathleen O'Neil

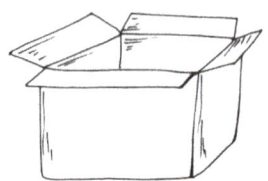

The Big Dog

Huldah and Andrew York

Andrew York, my great-grandfather died in 1913. His life of eighty years cast a large wine-colored shadow over my mom's side of the family, though my mom never even met him—she wasn't born until 1921. He was one of ten children and had nine children of his own. I am merely a drop in the large extended York family, on the tail end of his lineage.

The details we know come from research and writing that documented Andrew York's life. An ambitious and restless man, perhaps yearning to make it big, with ideas of adventure or fortunes out west, he always pivoted to the next best option—farming—at which he failed several times before his ultimate success with the York Mountain Winery in Templeton, California, one of the first wineries on the Coast. Andrew, was an accomplished, well-known early settler in the mountains south-west of Paso Robles, CA.

York Mountain Wine Label

Andrew York

1833 Born in Indiana to Pleasant and Rachel York, farmers of wheat, corn, alfalfa, and potatoes.

1852 The family moved to LaSalle, Il. Pleasant York farmed and raised cattle. He later found coal on his property and founded the Streator Coal Mining Company.

1854 Andrew and his brother Eli traveled to Nevada and California in a wagon train driving over 700 cattle, 50 horses and mules. After failing in the Nevada mines, they tried farming in California and landed in Napa. Eli settled there and later started a winery.

1860 Andrew married Louisa Long, a local Napa woman. They moved to St. Joseph, MO, purchased 120 acres to farm and started their family. In 1864, he enlisted to serve in the Civil War.

1865 After the Civil War, Andrew returned to California alone. Due to the American Indian Wars impeding his trip, he began a freight business for the U.S. Government between Julesburg, CO and Fort Kearny, NB.

1866 Andrew sold the freight business and traveled to the Cherokee nation where he received a claim for 160 acres in Baxter Springs, KS. He abandoned the claim after a few months of failing at farming. He returned home to his family.

1867 Andrew moved his family to Fannin County, TX. Where he farmed 60 acres. He and Louisa had two more children, now a family of six. Farming failed again.

1869–70 Andrew moved his family back to Missouri and purchased 200 acres in Granby. Another child, their fifth, was born.

1871 Tragedy struck when Andrew's home caught fire. His wife Louisa died, leaving him with five children to raise. He sold the farm and moved back to Napa, near his brother and family.

1873–1875 Andrew made his way down the coast by boat to San Luis Obispo, CA with his five children, to find land for farming. He met Huldah Matthews Priest, a spunky woman, who had left and divorced her "fire and brimstone" husband back in Texas and had come out west with her two children.

1876 Andrew and Huldah decided to marry and merge their families, now seven children strong.

1877 Andrew and Huldah purchase a ranch in Cayucos, CA. In 1879, they had a child together (Lulu, my grandmother). In 1882, their last child was born. Now nine children strong.

1882 The York's purchased 112 acres in the Santa Lucia Mountains, northeast of Cayucos and began farming, growing grapes, the Zinfandel varietal.

1895 The Ascension Winery was established and soon after renamed York Winery, and later York Mountain Winery.

1902 The winery produced 40,000 gallons of wine per year.

1913 Andrew York died. The York sons continued operating the winery until 1970 when it was sold outside the family.

1916 Huldah York died.

My grandparents, Lulu and Timothy O'Neil lived just down the hill from the winery and York family home, where they raised grapes, cherries and their family, the O'Neil clan. Mom often shared her childhood stories and fond, idealistic memories of their rural life.

Andrew and Huldah York's residence on York Mountain (the winery and vineyards are also on the property). Approximately, 1903 or 1904, Percy (child from Lulu's first marriage), Lulu, Andrew and Huldah seated, and Uncle Silas.

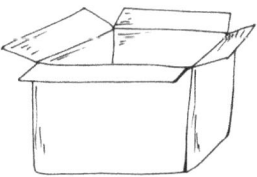

Little Dog

Family names are a strange thing, only passing down on the father's line in the family tree. Women's histories get lost, and sometimes they do too. But this is a story about a man— a father and legacy lost, either by his own doing or unfortunate circumstances.

John Molder (or Molier), born in 1780 in North Carolina, married **Rachel York** and had a son, Pleasant—my great-great grandfather.

He lived a short life, died at 30 in Grainger, TN. If he only knew that his name should have been carried on in our family legacy. But Rachel's father, Semore York II, saw to it that his grandchild Pleasant would take the York name, not Molder. Clearly, a snub to John who either abandoned his wife Rachel or did not meet the approval of the York male legacy.

If only he knew there was a winery in California possibly missing his name!

Will of Semore York Jr, 1819

I Semore York of the County of Grainger in the State of Tennessee being sick and like to die but of perfect mind and memory knowing that it is appointed for all men once to die Do make constitute and ordain this my Last Will and Testament and first of all I give and commend my Soul into the hands of God that give it and my Body to be buried in a desent and Christian Burial nothing doubting but I shall receive the same again in Judgment of the greate day by the mighty power of God. And as it related to the good things of this life with which it hath pleased God to bless me with in this world I give and bequeath in the following manner and form

Item 1st - It is my will that Uriah Yourk my son, Rachel Molder my Daughter, Sylvania Wood my Daughter, Enoch York My Son, Polly Deaton, Marthy Johnson My Daughters, and John York My Son have in addition to what they ~~have~~ already have received one Dollar each.

Item 2nd - it is my will that my wife Ann live on my plantation and have all the profits there of for the use of raising and schooling my children while she all remain my widow.

Item 3rd - It is my will that my wife have the benefit and increase of all my live stock and all my house hold furniture and farming uetentials During her widowhood for the use of Raising and scholling my said children as above named.

Item 4th - It is my will that my Daughter Sary and Elijah (Elizabeth?) each of them have a cow & calf and a good suit of Sunday clouths also a feather bed and bed furniture for each of them, whenever they become eighteen years of age.

Item 5th - It is my will that my sons Riley and Harrison each of them have a good sute of Sunday clothes a horse Bridle and Saddle whenever they become twenty one years of age.

Item 6th - It is my will that should my wife Ann marry after my death, then all my personal goods and chattels be sold and equally divided between her & the four children here in after named that is to say Sarah Elizabeth Riley & Harrison but not till my youngest child becomes of age.

Item 7th - It is my will that at the marriage or death of my said wife then my land be equally divided between my sons Riley & Harrison all but four acres which I have sold and layd off to John Wood adjoining his field near the mountain.

Item 8th - It is my will that my grandson Pleasant the son of my Daughter Rachel should he stay and remain with my wife till he be twenty one years of age that he have good shooling a good horse Saddle & Bridle and a good suit of Sunday Clothes out of my Said Estate.

Item 9th - I appoint my beloved Wife Ann and John Wood the Executor & Executrix of this my last Will and Testament, revoking all others ratifying and confirming this my last Will & Testament and no other in testimony where of I have here unto set my hand and seal this Seventh day of February 1819.

His mark
Seamore X York (Seal)

Signed and sealed & delivered

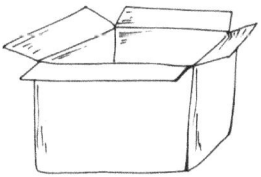

Lulu

Lulu

I never met her, my grandmother—Mom's mom. Her name was **Louisa** (oddly also the name of her father's first wife). But she was called Lulu, or later in life, her grandmotherly name, Gaga. Lulu was the last daughter born into the large York blended family, followed by a brother, the last son. My mom was the youngest of Lulu's five children—the surprise, unexpected late child born to Lulu and her Irish husband Timothy, when Lulu was 40. Grandma Gaga died in 1958, a year before I came on the scene.

I love the name Lulu and Petula—the British women and their music of the 1960s. Every time I heard their songs, as a kid, it seems like we were on a long drive, somewhere in the middle of hot desolate nowhere on a family vacation. Camping trailer in tow, worn out car games and me, wedged between two annoying brothers in the backseat. Dad drove with the radio on and his cigarette hanging outside the window, as Mom gazed out at the beauty of the desert. When I'd hear Petula Clark's "Downtown", I was transported to an exciting place I could only fantasize about. A big city, fashion, lights, glamour, and romance. Lulu's "To Sir with Love", created a longing of a distant world and magical time in my imagination.

I wonder if the women who preceded me in my family ever had fantasies of a different life when they heard an old song, read poetry or literature, or saw an advertisement of an exquisite hat and pair of gloves. I think of that when I look at this picture of Lulu. A rare photo of an expectant woman, a farmer's wife, in the early 1900s. Did she even listen to music, other than church hymns? Or ever have a minute to sit and read just for pleasure? Were those glamorous ads only for fashionable women, city folk?

As she posed, could she see a distant fantasy cross the hillside landscape, or hear an inner calling she couldn't fathom? Did she feel beautiful and feminine? I hope so, because to me, she was. And her name was Lulu.

Irish Roots

Timothy O'Neill (O'Neil)
dropped 2nd "l" upon immigration

My grandfather **Timothy O'Neil**, Mom's dad, has only been a shadow in my life. He became a naturalized citizen on January 29, 1902 — coincidently the same day as my birthday, January 29. He died in 1935, when Mom was just 13. Her 5-year diary, the one wrapped in layers of *Do Not Enter* string, documents the actual day he died and the preparations thereafter.

May 17 Mama and Yancy went to see Daddy. Hiya came home & she has no more job. Grace came, but we had a real good supper.

May 18 Saturday. We went to town and the hospital. I think I know the graduation dress I want, the blue one.

May 19 Sunday. Daddy is dead. We went down this afternoon and he died, 5:30. I'm glad it's over with.

May 20 We went to town. Mama and I got some good clothes. Marguerite came home. The McGoldrick's will come tonite. Some of them will.

May 21 We went to town. There was a rosary tonite in the funeral parlor. Daddy looks so natural and peaceful in the coffin.

May 22 Daddy's funeral today, all Catholic. He was buried in the Catholic cemetery in Paso Robles. Kate, Mary Ann, and Hanna left.

According to Mom, her dad was a hard worker, always busy keeping a farm and family afloat for as long as he could, while living with a heart condition, a result of rheumatic fever he had as a child. I think she missed having a closer and longer relationship with him.

She always remembered her parents on May 19, but as years passed, she couldn't remember which one died that day. Her mom died years later, May 15, 1958.

Funeral Notice

Died

May 19, 1935

𝕿𝖎𝖒𝖔𝖙𝖍𝖞 𝕺' 𝕹𝖊𝖎𝖑

Aged 60 years, 11 months, 4 days.
Native of Ireland

Beloved husband of Lulu O'Neil of Templeton; father of: Helen, Marguerite, Doris and Yancy O'Neil of Templeton; brother of: Mrs. Roberts of Ireland; Patrick O'Neil of San Francisco; Mrs. Sarah Curtain of San Francisco, Mrs. James Mc-Goldrick of Petaluma; Mrs. Joseph Pareira of Dixon, Calif.

Rosary will be recited at Kuehl Funeral Home Tuesday evening at eight P. M. Funeral services will be held Wednesday at 9 A. M., at Paso Robles St. Rose Catholic Church, Father Leo Beacon officiating. Interment will be in Paso Robles Holy Cross Cemetery.

Relatives and friends invited to attend.

Looking through Mom's collection of photos, I'm reminded of the time, in the late 1970s, when Mom and her sisters made a trip to Ireland to locate their father's old home and place of birth. She saved a well-documented photo album of the pilgrimage to Bunclody, near Enniscorthy, in County Wexford, southern Ireland. It was a big deal for them. And for Mom, a single mother, almost impossible, as it was well out of her financial range. I recall the efforts made to help her make the trip. Family members chipped in. I was a college student and even scraped up $100 to donate. Her workmates at K-Mart also surprised her with a collection they pulled together. And of course, she saved everything she could to make her trip of a lifetime happen.

In the front of the photo album, she placed a poem probably written by my cousin Katherine who likely organized the event. Mom was known as "Bobis" by her family — a name she gave to herself as a young child. She was the baby of the family, and she pronounced it as Bobis. Later her nieces and nephews referred to her as "Auntie Bob".

```
                  ODE TO AUNTIE BOB

  For many long years, we've heard you three say,
  You'd all go to Eire together someday.
  You ain't gettin' younger, nor any more spry,
  So we'd like you to go before summer rolls by.


  We all chipped in, to give you these sums,
  Your neices, your nephews, your daughters, and sons.
  So get the ball rollin', line up and go,
  We're counting on you to spearhead this show.



We love you a lot, so have lots of fun,
Trod the old sod, leave nuthin' undone.
A swingin' good time is all that we ask,
If you do not go, we will take you to task'.
```

Ode to Auntie Bob

Most of the relatives on Mom's side of the family, other than immediate aunts, uncles, and cousins, are just distant names in our family history. There were many Yorks and O'Neils, a large collective clan of great-aunts and uncles I never met—nor have much knowledge of or photos to excavate.

On Memorial Days we paid our respects to the York gravesite. With flowers picked from our backyard, we made pretty springtime arrangements in aluminum wrapped coffee and orange juice cans, saved for the occasion. We'd drive up the coast to the cemetery in Cayucos, often with a packed picnic lunch. Mom would share her memories and stories over a cup of lemonade and a bologna sandwich after we decorated the graves.

Others in the family would tend to her father's gravesite, in Paso Robles, where he rests closer to his Catholic roots, but far away from his childhood Irish home.

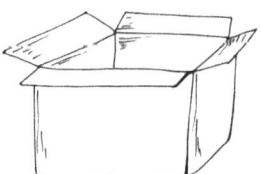

The Black Letter

O ne by one they came from Ireland to America for a better life. Perhaps forever. They came with a promise of hope and escape from the barren land. One by one, my great-grand-parents said good-bye to daughters going to be domestics in New York, and sons to forage a new life. From Ireland five of their offspring sailed away.

After time in Syracuse, NY, my grandfather, **Timothy O'Neil**, made his way to San Francisco where other family and siblings settled. A farmer and hardworking Catholic, he married Lulu, a divorced Protestant. Life was fruitful for the O'Neils, growing grapes and cherries, while raising their four children, in Templeton, just down the coast from San Francisco.

One day a letter came from Ireland. Important and edged in black. My mother's little girl eyes noticed it's heavy shadow of meaning for her father. Upon quietly reading the sad news of his mother's death, he disappeared for the day. After his return, nothing was ever said about the black letter. Life continued on.

Sample of a Mourning Stationery Envelope

Dad's Side
Rasgorsheks and Greenelshs

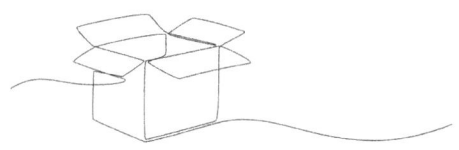

Dad's Side

RASGORSHEKS & GREENELSHS

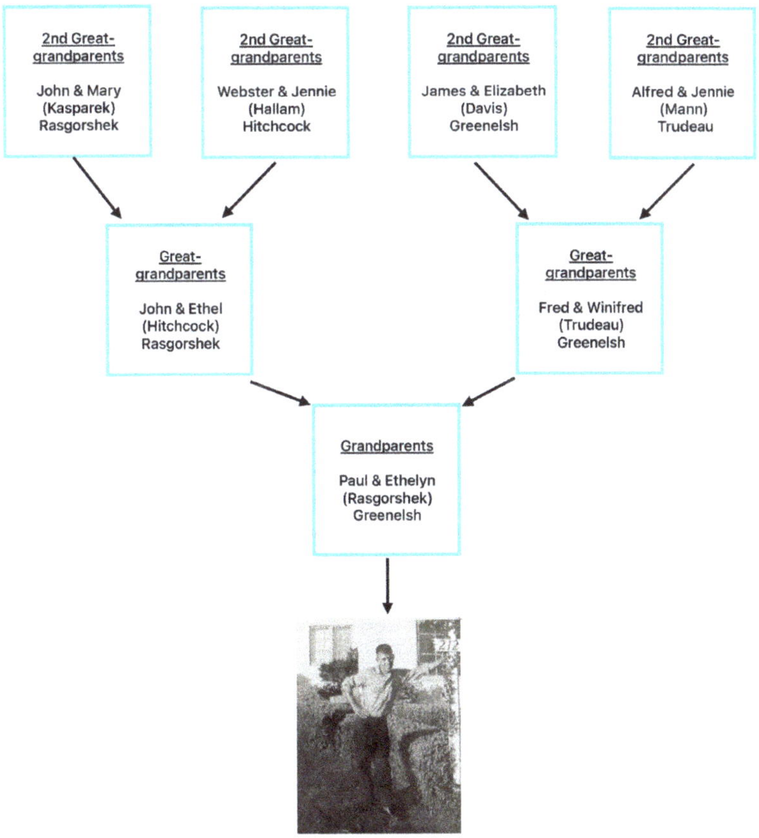

2nd Great-grandparents	2nd Great-grandparents	2nd Great-grandparents	2nd Great-grandparents
John & Mary (Kasparek) Rasgorshek	Webster & Jennie (Hallam) Hitchcock	James & Elizabeth (Davis) Greenelsh	Alfred & Jennie (Mann) Trudeau

Great-grandparents

John & Ethel (Hitchcock) Rasgorshek

Great-grandparents

Fred & Winifred (Trudeau) Greenelsh

Grandparents

Paul & Ethelyn (Rasgorshek) Greenelsh

Dad
Marvin Fred Greenelsh

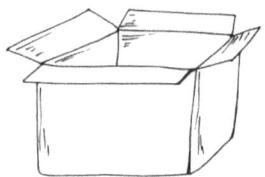

Death Do Us Part

John Rasgorshek

The family story, mostly true, **John Rasgorshek** the elder, my 2nd great-grandfather, was murdered. There are two unanswered mysteries and maybe unearthed secrets to this story.

The first of the Rasgorshek brothers, John, settled in a Bohemian enclave in Nebraska in 1876, a year before his younger brother Gabriel joined him, making Omaha and the surrounding area their home. Successful tailors, men of dreams and losses.

His first wife Mary, my 2nd great-grandmother, remains a mystery. An immigrant, ten years younger, they had five children, the first when she was 18. Four survived. The youngest, an infant, died at three months, February 1883 — Mary would have been 27. Little Frank's death announcement makes condolences only to John. It is unknown whether Mary died in childbirth or left. She just disappeared. No pictures, no death announcement, no gravesite.

At Plattsmouth, February 3, infant son of John Rasgorshek, aged three months.

Lincoln Nebraska State Journal 1883

John, who had means, left no loveable, traceable goodbye to Mary. He remarried and had five more children.

John's well-documented death was the result of a beating he took by three thugs a month before succumbing to his injuries at the age of 60, March 1907. After investigators chased down all clues, they concluded he was a victim of mistaken identity for an undetermined reason. Jewelry and money were not taken.

We will never know what truly went down that night or any relevant back story. But a family lost a father, husband, and brother too soon.

MAY DIE FROM BEATING

M. A. Rasgorshek is Set Upon by Three Men On His Way Home.

Special to the Press.

Omaha, Feb. 2.—M. A. Rasgorshek, who conducts a tailoring establishment at 510 South Thirteenth street was set upon by thugs on his way home, on Friday night and given a terrible beating.

Shortly after 9 o'clock Rasgorshek left a Farnam street car at Thirty-fifth street. While crossing an alley between Douglas and Farnam streets, three men jumped on him and rendered him unconscious by striking him upon the head with some instrument.

When he regained consciousness he was lying in a pool of blood.

The assault was evidently not made for the purpose of robbery, for a valuable watch and several dollars in change were not taken.

Mr. Rasgorshek was conscious only at short intervals during the night. It is feared that his injuries may prove fatal. He was evidently mistaken for someone else.

Nebraska Daily Press 1907

RASGORSHEK DIES; SLUGGING FATAL

Victim of Mistaken Identity Beaten Night of February 1 Succumbs to Injuries.

Commission Man Who Had Incurred Ill-Will Is Believed to Have Been Meant for Victim.

Evening World Herald 1907

John's beating, follow up newspaper stories, and his death made headlines in all the local papers. It was investigated and reported. His life celebrated. His loss forever remembered.

But for Mary — nothing.

JOHN RASGORSHEK DIES OF WOUNDS

Well-Known Omahan, Who Was Assaulted by Thugs, Succumbs to Injuries.

ASSAILANTS ARE UNKNOWN

John Rasgorshek, 307 North Twenty-fifth street, after battling for his life since February 1, died this morning from the effects of a terrible beating given him by unknown thugs on that date.

For ten days after the assault, Mr.

John Rasgorshek.

Rasgorshek was unconscious and it was not then thought he could recover. He then began to improve, and was able to be about his room, until Sunday, when a turn for the worse came.

Mr. Rasgorshek could give no accurate description of his assailants. He declared there were three of them, all young men. The police took up the slender clue, but could not find the assailants.

Mr. Rasgorshek, who was 60 years old, is survived by a wife and nine children, Elsie, Mary, Margaret, Edward, Henry, William and Mrs. Josephine Oteson of Omaha, and Fred and John of Los Angeles.

Definite funeral arrangements will not be made until the two absent sons are heard from.

The police assert that the attack on Mr. Rasgorshek was a case of mistaken identity, as he was not known to have enemies and there was no attempt to rob him after he had been beaten into insensibility.

Obituary for John Rasgorshek

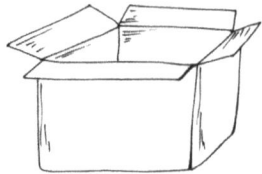

Where Are You Mary?

Dear **Mary**,

I can't let go of this need to contact you. An inner voice keeps whispering a tender nudge. Perhaps it's just my wishful thinking wanting to resolve your mystery. There's only a trace of evidence that you once lived — the fact that you are the mother of my great-grandfather John. Do you remember your son Johnnie?

I have this nagging feeling you have a story to tell. My guess, it wasn't happy. So, if you get a chance in your busy afterlife schedule, I want to hear from you. Can you possibly channel a clue or two — drop something into my consciousness or mysteriously land a curious tip into my lap? Here are a few questions I've been wondering about. Please tell me more.

1. *I know you were born, circa 1854, in Austria, probably in Bohemia. Is your maiden name Kasperak or Casparek?*

2. *I know you came to the U.S., but I'm not sure when, or why. Did your brother Augustus come with you?*

3. *I think you were a wife, but don't know if, when or where you were married. Your presumed husband, my great-great-grandfather, John Rasgorshek was ten years your senior. Did you meet and marry around 1873 in New Haven, Connecticut? Why did you move to Plattsmouth, Nebraska?*

4. *I know you had five children, starting at age 18. Your fourth was my great-grandfather, born in 1880, also named John. Your known last born, Frank, died as an infant, just three months old, in 1883. He has a grave and an obituary, but only your husband John was acknowledged as the father. Where are you?*

5. *You seem to disappear. Did you die then too? Did you leave? Or were you sent away?*

6. *You don't have a grave at all. If you died, why didn't your husband provide for your burial? If not, where did you go, and why?*

7. *A child, Fred, was born in 1884. Was he yours? Or was it your husband's next wife?*

8. *Your husband John, remarried in 1887. They had more children.*

9. *And he was murdered (1907). Did you have anything to do with that?*

I patiently await your response.

Love,

Your great-great-granddaughter

Jennie's Watch

Jennie Hallam Hitchcock

A time piece —
and a life I know so little about,
my great-great-grandmother.

A gold pocket watch —
A treasured trinket.
Perhaps a loving gift,
with your name *Jennie*
etched in gold laced memories.

A piece of time —
your family must have grieved.
You and your new baby's untimely death.
A husband, and three precious ones
missing your nurturing beat.

Your timepiece closed too soon.

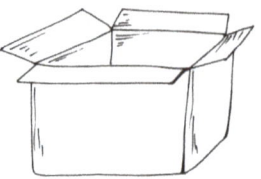

Ethel's Photo Album
and Bible

Ethel's Photo Album

E xquisite, fragile, old, once ornate, special, and loved. In these pages you once touched, remembered, treasured, yearned over, and stored away—if only these pictures could talk. I feel their presence, a mystery of dear memories—whispering. I am listening for you to guide me along. For your past is my past. Your stories, my stories.

Peacock blue velvet and a wood lacquered, floral embossed cover with a porcelain faced Victorian lady; gold edged pages and a tooled brass latch that once held together what is now barely together. So fancy, for an unfancy woman. The early life of my great-grandmother, **Ethel May Hitchcock Rasgorshek**— her collected memories in a delicate old relic.

Ethel's Photo Album

Ethel as a Child

Deep set dark eyes, long thick, waist-length, wavy brunette hair, one photo I know is a younger you. With careful excavation of each photo I can wiggle out without tearing mounted edges, I look for prize clues—a name, date or sweet note—mostly blank, all from the 1800s. Many unknown faces and funeral cards, stoic and solemn, a few little hints—small resemblances in eyes or noses and in the almost smiles that invite me to come back and visit another time.

Various Family Portraits

I may never know the distant cousins, your old schoolmates, or neighbors. But I can get to know more about you and how you cared for those you loved. Pieces of stories, and mysteries to explore will keep me going, to imagine and feel your presence. I'll journey back into your precious photo album again one day, for another visit—and listen for more whispers within these pages.

 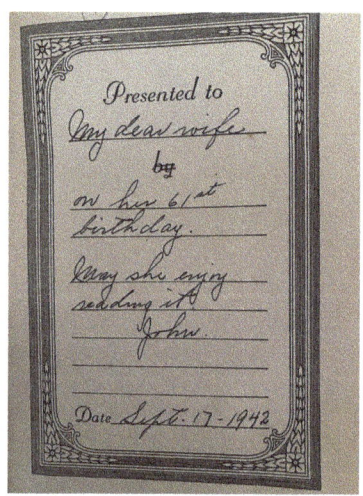

Ethel's Bible Gifted by Her Husband John

Unlike your ornate photo album, the Bible, black with gold lettering, is not fancy. A gift from your husband, I'm amused at the inscription. *Presented to: My dear wife, on her 61st birthday. May she enjoy reading it, John. Sept. 17, 1942.* I can think of more enjoyable gifts, but I'm sure it was a gift of love. The Bible is worn and beloved with little memories tucked between pages—the newspaper clipping with his picture from the announcement of his prestigious appointment and most notably a newspaper clipping of John's obituary from 1947.

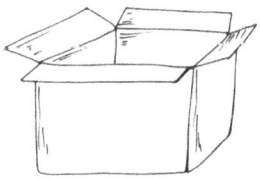

Johnnie's Letters

John Rasgorshek and Ethel Hitchcock

T he letters are 123 years old! Dated July–Sept 1900, two years before my great-grandparents **John Rasgorshek and Ethel Hitchcock** were married June 25, 1902. I can't believe I have such treasures found in a plastic bag of items my aunt Gloria gave me a couple of years ago.

The stack of folded lined letter paper yellowed and fragile with time. It's a slow read, pages of faded pencil handwriting, but I'm excited to hear his voice and words. I grab a magnifying glass and make a pot of tea.

 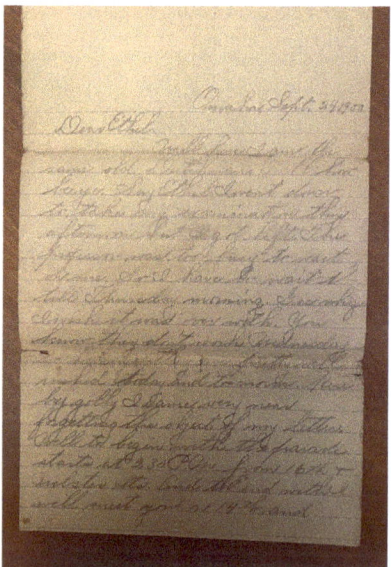

Johnnie's Letters

Johnnie was 20 years old in 1900 and Ethel was 19. They both lived in Omaha, Nebraska, she in Ward 6 and he in Ward 9. Letter writing was the common means to communicate with one another. Notes, often long, were a review of ordinary daily life, but I learned a few things about my great-grandfather.

He was a working-class son of a tailor, but his spelling and grammar were pretty good. A social young man about town, he smoked and drank a bit, perhaps a little more with Ethel being away. Her mother died just a year earlier, and my guess, she may have been visiting in Wisconsin, where her mother's side of the family, the Hallams lived. Johnnie was talkative and seems gossipy at times. He worked hard as a tinner (so he says), canning fruit for a local company. But clearly just to get paid so he could go out with his friends. Not very romantic, at least in this stage of their relationship, here are some random excerpts.

I received your last letter about a half an hour ago and thought I might as well sit down and answer it now, as I have nothing else to do.

———

Well after work I came home and dressed up and went downtown and met Walter. Well, we stood on the corner smoking when Lora, Alice, Ethel, Bob, and Mr. Blue from Blair came up. We held down the corner for over an hour. About 10, the girls left us, and we went in the cigar store on the corner and played slot machines for about 15 minutes.

———

Well, we left the store and who should we meet but the girls accompanied by Grace and some fellow. I got home at 12 and didn't know anything till a quarter of 12 next morning. Talk about sleep, what do you think of it. I ate dinner and decided to spend a quiet afternoon alone at Hanscom. I was sitting on the pavilion enjoying an afternoon smoke when I felt somebody pull my chair turning around, I saw The Honorable

Mr. Black and Mr. Blue so we went out for a stroll around Lover's Lane and then we went over on the Westside and sat down. We sat there for about an hour and who do you think came strolling up towards us. There was Grace, Lora, Ethel, Daisy Barker, Alice, Pearl Norman's cousin and some other girl I forgot her name.

————

The whole bunch of us went to Lora's house and had quite a time. I got to singing "I've Lost Ma Baby" and I turned around and saw everybody laughing, so I quit and asked what they were laughing about, when Bob said, didn't you lose her yesterday? Say Ethel, to tell the truth, I couldn't enjoy myself much after.

————

I told him that I knew nothing about it . . . he thought maybe I could find out something. Gee whiz, you'd ought to have heard me rip into him. I wasn't no walking newspaper.

————

Well, we worked until 7 pm. You'd ought to have seen me ditch currants they gave B. Van Deusen and me 16 boxes to pick and told us we could go home when we got through, so I sent and ditched 3 boxes down in the elevator hole.

————

The bandstand was raised about three feet above the platform and the dam fool that built it didn't brace it at all. Well about three o'clock, Lora, Bob, Ethel and I were standing near there and we heard a howl and a crash and turning around we couldn't see no bandstand. All you could see was a mix up of boards, men, instruments, music racks and sheet music. I had to laugh at my brother he was playing then when the crash came. Well Golly Gee he turned a back somersault right over the back of his chair and hit the top of his brow. Well I ran over and asked if he was hurt. He asked if I had seen his glasses. Well I looked at him and had to laugh right in his face because he had his glasses on.

———————

We got over to the house and met your father downstairs. He hadn't had any supper, so Grace went up and cooked a cup of tea and say we had a swell supper. I sat there talking to your father until 11:15 and then left for home.

———————

Say Ethel I hope you will forgive me for using that language in that last letter of mine, but I didn't think anything of it at the time I wrote it. I see now I did wrong. Say hun you had better come back to Omaha as soon as you can...

———————

Well, I'll have to close this would be letter with the usual xxxx. Goodnight from your loving friend, "Johnnie".

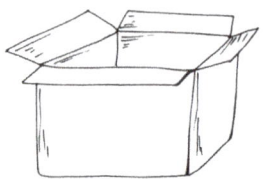

Wilted Rose

Ethelyn

Aroaring and rambling 1920s vibe Grandma, **Ethelyn** had flapper girl looks with deep-set made-up eyes and a short wavy hairdo. A young girl swooped up in the day, playing saxophone in an all-female jazz band. Concerts and dances in Los Angeles ballrooms and Catalina's Casino — far more interesting than the occasional recitals her mother held at her family home, a two-and-a-half-acre poultry ranch on Chandler Blvd. in the San Fernando Valley.

Born in Boyle Heights, 1908, named Ethelyn, by her mother Ethel and father John Rasgorshek she presumably had a happy childhood. In old photos, wearing charming little dresses and enormous bows in her hair, she appeared well cared for and well loved. Petite with big blue-grey piercing eyes and thick brown wavy hair — she never thought she had good teeth. "Our family didn't get good teeth," she'd say. But she was cute and pretty in her own way.

Ethelyn on the Beach

She wasn't a dusty rose, but maybe one that wilted too soon. When I would visit Grandma, she would always show off some new modern dress she purchased, on sale of course, with matching high heels. And she loved movie magazines. We played cards as she shared some celebrity tidbit, stating a *National Enquirer* fact that a well-known high-gloss beauty had bad skin, just like me, a young pimple-plagued teen, mastering Gin Rummy or Canasta on a balmy summer night. She tossed out bits of wisdom and updates about her life; the benefit of the new polyester double-knit wash and wear, or the status of her rheumatism.

The stories that Grandma didn't share were notable — maybe too shameful, full of regret or too racy, in her mind, to expose around me, or anyone. The stoic, stiff upper lip, keep-things-to-yourself family culture. She must have experienced such excitement and glamour playing the saxophone and being a part of an all-female jazz band performing around LA. I can only imagine the rush, somewhere between taboo and breaking a musical glass ceiling for the time. The fun, fantasy, gossip, and glamour, at least in this granddaughter's eyes and imagination, full of questions. Where did her talent and love for music come from? Or the fact that she became pregnant in high school, during a time when young girls made mysterious extended visits to aunts who lived out of town.

Grandma glowed in pictures with her first teenage love — her music man. They married to legitimize their child and then annulled it. Perhaps he was the love of her life, but her father, John Rasgorshek made sure, with a threat and a rifle, that her

Grandma and Her Music Man

music man would never come around again. Of course, John did not own a rifle.

No one ever spoke of her second marriage with a handsome milkman. The big glamorous wedding, surrounded by family, friends, bridesmaids and groomsmen—a pristine 8 x 10, no dust. It was a short marriage with no clue as to why it ended. And then there was husband number three, my grandfather. Ethelyn worked with him at the gas company, as a stenographer. They had family mid-west roots in common, but they were quite different. I can't help but think that this was the beginning of her wilting years, 1935.

Grandpa was stern, responsible, and rigid, but he liked a good laugh, when he wasn't upset about something. There was a part of him that had wilted too, I expect—a previous marriage, a daughter, and perhaps a lighter life and mood in earlier days. Grandma was a city girl at heart but he loved the outdoors, a western cowboy at heart. They bought a ranch in Newhall, just north of LA, started a poultry business, and had two sons. Grandma became a full-time mom, living back on a poultry ranch. The music died and the jazzy glamourous life left to that in movie magazines.

The stories and secrets not told continued. To what extent my grandma knew of Grandpa's other life and future legal, criminal, problems, I'll never know. But it gave her a lot to worry about—a deep secret no doubt keeping her awake at night. Perhaps she soothed herself with a distant life in the radio, worlds away, where she kept her music and memories.

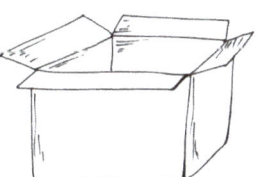

John Norman

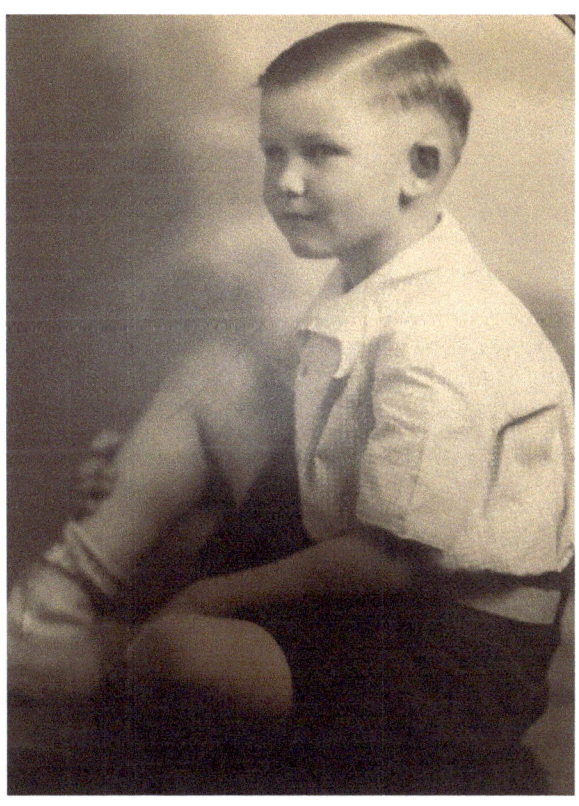

John Norman

We called him **Norm**, though he was known as John outside of the family. For whatever reason, my grandmother doubled down, naming two of her sons John, one in 1925 and one in 1940, after her dad and his dad — both John Rasgorshek.

Uncle Norm, born in 1925, had a good, but perhaps unusual childhood. He was the third John Rasgorshek in the family lineage, at least through his school age years, raised by his grandparents, who he called Mom and Dad. His sister, he was told, was in fact his mother!

Barely 16 in 1924, his birth mother, my grandmother Ethelyn, revealed an indiscretion and imminent little one. No doubt, her parents were dismayed, and a plan was made. She took an absence from high school and married her beau in another county, for secretive and legitimizing purposes. But the marriage wasn't really a marriage and John Norman didn't take his father's name — until he had to.

He had an inkling that the mom-sister, sister-mom situation wasn't quite right. Ethelyn wanted him back upon her second marriage in 1932, but the grandparents said No. Several years later, at 12 years old, he was finally told, what he thought he knew might be true — his sister was his mother.

He was a quiet man with a dry sense of humor, like Ethelyn and a lanky stature, perhaps like his father, 5'9" and 125 lbs. at age 18.

The WW2 draft came calling as did his official name, resisted by Norm but required by the Army. John Norman Roth served his country bravely, earning a bronze star.

Roth Given Bronze Star Medal

Back in the days of the Belgian Bulge, a Valley boy, Pfc. Norman Roth, Infantry, grandson of Mr. and Mrs. John Rasgorshek, 12959 Chandler Blvd., was catapulted into the midst of battle upon hitting the shores of France.

After seeing action there with the 7th Army his regiment crossed the Rhine into Germany. Roth writes that they made quite a tour of Germany on the outside of a tank, taking over one town after another as they progressed.

The going was not always easy and his friends are proud of the fact that he has now been awarded the Bronze Star Medal for "heroic achievement in action" back in April near Wablingen, Germany. His citation further reads:

"Private Roth, disregarding the enemy action, ran forward toward the hostile positions, diverting the fire of the opposing troops to himself, and thus by his courageous action enabled his companions to outflank the enemy position, killing four of the hostile soldiers."

He is now stationed with the occupation troops in the vicinity of Heidelberg.

SEES ACTION — Pfc. Norman Roth, Valley youth now in Germany, who has received Bronze Star Medal for heroic achievement.

Burglarize Home

Morris M. Leffer reported to police that a burglar took a $70 revolver and $82.50 worth of jewelry from his home at 17129 Ventura Blvd.

John Roth Given Bronze Star

The Rasgorshek name, on our line of the family came to an end. But, the family's John-naming tradition marched on. My grandmother had a third marriage and two more boys, Marvin, and her 2nd John.

Missing the Everyday

Letters to Uncle Norm

Time to start hunting again. I grab the plastic bag that contains a collection of old cards and letters **Aunt Gloria** gave me. My **uncle Norm** saved them from his WW2 service in the Army. These were important to him, therefore important to me too – worthy of another pot of tea and an otherwise free afternoon.

Gloria hung on to all the treasured love letters she sent him – I wish those were here too. I have the collection of cards and letters from fall 1946 to sometime after Easter 1947, from Fort Sill, Oklahoma, though his service began in 1944 in Germany, France, and Ft. Hood, TX.

Clearly, family and friends cared about Norman and were looking forward to his return home in the spring of 1947. They often referred to letters and cards he had sent them. But the correspondence gives more of a glimpse into the Rasgorshek home life in Van Nuys, CA, and his buddy from school, rather than Norman's experiences or state of mind.

The notes from his army friends, talk of finding their way back to civilian life yet seemed to miss a bit of the brotherhood connection and sense of purpose.

At home, life was simple and provided the comfort of the familiar.

From Dad (Johnnie, John Rasgorshek)

. . . I have the clipping from the Times about the UCLA Nebraska game played here yesterday. I sent the clippings of the USC & UCLA game last week. Did you get it? I have had some pretty bad days since you left, especially Sunday and today . . . I bought a Philo radio at the Broadway, they had advertised, we phoned and got the last one, but when they

took it off the floor, they saw that the cabinet had cracked. . . . The radishes are all up. Mother just told me she found the onion sets and set out 2 rows. Is Fort Sill further from home than Camp Hood?

From Mother (Ethel)

. . . Well, I'll try to finish this letter, your dad is too sick to finish it. I am sitting in a chair writing but I guess you can make it out. I washed today and am tired tonight . . . You be careful and look out for yourself. If you don't no one will . . . Go to church one of these Sunday's, it will do you good. You find the best fellows going to church. You notice the Catholic boys never miss church, they were brought up to go to church. When you get older you will wish you had . . . With love and best wishes, Dad and Mother

From various aunts and uncles (Josie, Susie and Otto, Margie and Fred)

Dear Norman, How are you? . . . How do you like Ft. Sill? . . . We have had very foggy weather here . . . everyone here is just about the same . . . Went up to Newhall to get a turkey. Ethel and Paul were both pretty busy. I do hope they sell most of their turkeys, it's such a job to raise them . . . News is scarce here. Will be glad to hear from you.

Hope you have a nice Christmas . . . Looking for a tree they seem so high 3 & 4.50 out here & not nice bushy one just tall skimpy ones. Wish you could be home around the tree. . . . Best wishes and good health.

Hope you have a nice Easter. Guess we'll have a leg of lamb. Now take care of yourself and write when you can . . .

Here's wishing you a very Happy Birthday. Hope you will go have a little treat on me. Wish it could be more but it will go a little way . . . had quite an earthquake yesterday a.m. . . . are you near the tornado, that sure was terrible, pictures are in the Times . . . The fog has lifted. We had some sunshine today but still cold.

From Ethelyn (his sister and biological mother)

Dear Norman, Received your letter and was so glad to hear that you are feeling better. Was home yesterday. Dad just the same. He is looking forward to your getting home for good. It is raining today . . . Marvin wonders if you got his letter? Try to write him. He would be so pleased . . . Didn't send you anything for your birthday as you will be coming home soon . . . you will be needing some clothes . . . Dad said it was just 20 more days. He has been so miserable. Must close for now. Hope to see you soon. Lots of love.

From his best friend (Cliffe)

December 17th, Hollywood

Dear Norm . . . Things have been happening for me, fast and furious. All good . . . one night who do you think should come over but Bob, civilian Bob that is . . . He was dressed like a million. We asked him where he got the beautiful sport coat and he showed us the label "Made in Nuremberg, Germany" . . . he has had the time of his life over there. He was radio operator on the C-54 that took Justice Jackson of the Nuremberg Trials all over Europe to big dinners given in Jackson's honor . . . And did Bob come back with the loot. He has three pairs of German binoculars one of which he let me use at the Green Bay-Ram game. They brought the game right into our laps. You think I'm kidding, I could see Waterfield needed a shave. Incidentally Rams won 38-17 . . . He also got a camera . . . Three photograph albums have already been filled . . . Man has he got stories to tell . . . I don't know why I never thought of doing this before. By the time you get this I will have dubbed copies of Dick's records. My new store-boughten records are Count Basie's "Mutton-Leg". Glen Miller's "Little Brown Jug" – finally got it. Benny Goodman's "Rattle and Roll". Last of all, good news from the Studio. Their Christmas present to me was making me foreman of the shipping room with a raise in pay, NATCH!! . . . Well Norm, it's about 10 o'clock so I think I better sign off. Write some more. Merry Xmas

I still wonder why Uncle Norm kept these letters all these years. No doubt a significant chapter in his life—one of change and personal challenge. They marked the everyday homelife he missed that might never be the same again. He had become a man, with experiences he never spoke of, including that which earned him the Bronze Star. His dad waited for his return and sadly died a short time thereafter, June 27, 1947.

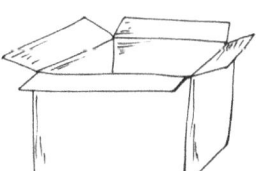

Unfinished Business

B ack sitting on my meditation cushion and ready to dig into another part of the family history journey.

I start with the brown grocery bag. I pull out a letter addressed to me in Dec. 2008 from my aunt Bonnie's husband on his business stationary, thanking me for the Christmas card and informing me that Bonnie had died over a year prior in Nov. 2007.

She was very fond of you, and I wish you the best.

I was fond of Bonnie too. Sadly, she had been estranged from her father (my grandfather on the Greenelsh side) for most of her adult life. The note makes me sad too.

Now, I get to old photos. Several in old frames. And I see Aunt Gloria's note.

Can you use these?

It's an assortment she gave me, more from the Rasgorshek side of the family. More lives to scour and mysteries to solve.

And like many of the old black and white photos, the information on the back, if any, is cryptic.

Jennie Hallam Hitchcock (r)

The back of the photo notes only a date, July 1883. Fortunately, I believe the woman on the right to be my great-great- grandmother, **Jennie Hallam Hitchcock**. I wonder if the timepiece in her pocket is the one, I have (see Jennie's Watch). I have no idea who the other woman is, perhaps one of her sisters.

Up next, a childhood picture of my grandmother. And, perfectly noted on the back, *Merry Christmas and Happy New Year to Cousin Ethelyn from Edwin, December 1923*. The picture was probably taken several years earlier, perhaps by him, and clearly a sweet gift. As always, my grandma is so nicely dressed, topped with a fabulous bow!

 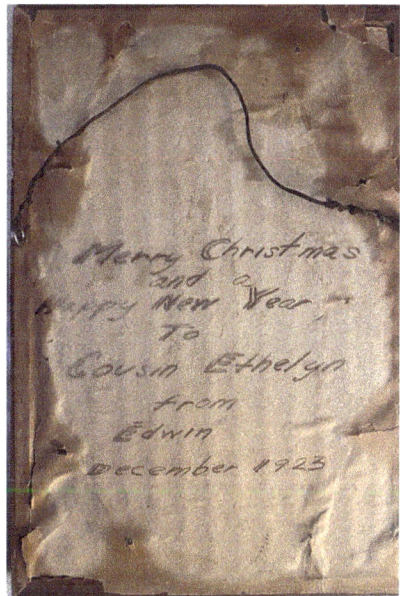

Childhood Photo of My Grandmother Ethelyn

I make my way through the rest of the stack of old photos. Ones from the 1800s intrigue me, but some will remain a mystery, at least for now.

And there's one last envelope, Railroad Notes from Arthur Hitchcock, my great-uncle. This could be a fascinating read—if I can get through 17 legal size pages of his detailed narrative.

The document, *The Effect of the Diesel Electric Locomotive on the Engineer's Job*, dated July 1943 is a historical perspective from his employment beginning in 1910 with the Chicago and Northwestern Railway.

I bag up everything again, except Grandma's picture. How quickly a life goes by and becomes a just collection of stuff, remnants of hard work, and maybe unfinished business.

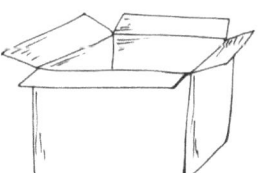

Looking Up

Gabriel Rasgorshek

I 'd like to think he was a profound thinker in addition to being the most intriguing man, in my assortment of relatives. An immigrant, a tailor, patented inventor, a painter, a magician, brother, husband, father, victim of a scandalous cheating wife — and overall mystery man of many accomplishments, losses and complexity.

Seemingly he had the ability to look up and move forward. Chasing his rising and setting sun, emotionally escaping the past, he continued moving his life west, from the old Austrian Empire to New Haven, CN, Omaha and Plattsmouth, NB and lastly to Los Angeles.

In his early days as a magician (and possibly a participant in the trickery on those with broken hearts), he was known for his expertise with psychic mediums on how spirit portraits could be produced on canvases in their mysterious stage productions. Later, in unsubstantiated family stories, he studied with Houdini. More fact based, in his retirement years, he performed magic shows at ladies' club luncheons.

> **Next Sunday Night.**
> Rasgorshek vs. Hume—The latter's "spirits" exposed by the former, at Love's opera house next Sunday night. Rasgorshek will reproduce Dr. Hume's entire program, first privately as did Hume then publicly in order that the audience may see just how it is done. No turning low of lights but every trick performed open and above board. Be there! Admission, adults 25 cents; children 10 cents; gallery 15 cents. 4-4t

Freemont Tribune 1891

Gabe the Magician

I think of **Uncle Gabe** looking down at me as I explore his life, not knowing his 2nd great-niece, perhaps perplexed at my interest in his life.

An esoteric canvas in my imagination, I wish I could look up at his spirit portrait and ask him these questions:

1. *Are you from Graz, Austria, Slovenia, or Hungary?*

2. *Did your mother bring you and your brother John to America after your father died?*

3. *Did an older brother (or cousin), Lorenzo, stay behind? Why did you come?*

4. *Were family or friends already in Nebraska?*

5. *Where did you meet your wife, Ada? Was it love at first sight?*

6. *Tell me about your children. Your oldest son was an actor, but died at age 31? How did you and Ada survive the loss of your twins who died at childbirth? Did your eldest daughter die while giving birth?*

7. *And the affair? Why do you think Ada cheated? She was scammed, but also so very willing to leave you, according to the newspaper articles. How did you survive such humiliation?*

8. *Were you together when Ada died?*

9. *How did you and your brother John become tailors? Was your dad a tailor too?*

10. *Tell me about John, my great-great-grandfather. Was he a good man? Can you tell me how his first wife Mary, my great-great-grandmother, died? Or did she leave?*

11. *What can you tell me about the night John was accosted? Did he suffer much before he died? You must have missed him terribly.*

12. *How or why did you invent the cover for an opening in stovepipes in 1884?*

13. *When did you start painting? Do you know that I have two of them in my home? Were the landscapes of your childhood? Was it happy? Why are all the flowers in your still life's falling or wilting out of vases? Was that a fashionable thing, or illustrating your sadness?*

14. *And when and why did you become a magician? My uncle Norm liked it when you showed him magic tricks when he was a kid. He thought you were a kind man. Were you?*

15. *And did you ever meet or study with Houdini? Did you look up to him, like I look up to you?"*

As I fantasize about a legitimate medium channeling truthworthy answers to all my questions, I look at his paintings. I will never know all there is to know, but I'm inspired and will keep looking up.

> Ghost show for sale, cheap; best ever built. Gabe Rasgorshek, 1415 Douglas street. 3536-x2

Omaha World Herald 1906

Uncle Gabe

Ada, Is This You?

Ada?

Ada, your life may just be a note assigned to Uncle Gabe's history — his spouse, born in England, or New York, 1861, and died in Omaha, 1916, at 55, sadly after all four of your children had passed away. The photograph, neatly and simply framed with a piece of red thread connecting two small tacks in the back, and your noteworthy newspaper articles intrigue me. Looking and thinking about your life makes me realize that amongst the unknown or understood facts, your life has something to say.

I can only imagine circumstances that led you to your sultry adventure in the late summer days in August 1896. Were you bored, lonely or just daring?

Gabe arose one morning to chaos: a burglary, his gold watch, a chain, and money missing. The old house in disarray on one of those days when it would get very hot again, especially for you Ada, having staged the burglary, to hide your secret — a torrid affair. As the newspaper story goes — you confessed to the "fatherly" detective; his investigative eye had seen this scam before.

According to the local rag, a *wily intruder with suave and fetching manners* started coming around for illicit encounters on those scorching, lonely summer days. Did he really steal your heart, one ventricle at a time? The scheme against your liege lord, otherwise known as your loyal boring husband Gabe, backfired. You were duped by a horse-trading, hot, blond, mustached lover, as was the plan to *fly with the wings of love* to a new, more exciting life in Minneapolis.

Were you just naïve, selfish, or sad when the heat eroded your commitment and common sense?

Ada, was that really you? I have deduced that it probably might be.

A lone soul.

ELOPEMENT FRUSTRATED.

Mrs. Rasgorshek Steals Her Husband's Watch to Raise Funds.

The burglary of the Rasgorshek household at 805 North Twentieth street Tuesday night is no longer a mystery. By her own confession, Mrs. Rasgorshek is guilty of robbing her husband of a gold watch and chain, valued at $80, and $12 in money. It happened this way:

For several years Gabriel, who is a tailor, and his wife, Ada, have lived together in unalloyed domestic bliss. About five months ago, a wily intruder with suave and fetching manners and carefully waxed blond moustache, entered the Rasgorshek home and proceeded ruthlessly to occupy one by one the auricles and ventricles of the woman's heart, and when all four compartments finally became his, she clung to him with a devotion that would not be thwarted. Joseph Skeleton, for that is the "masher's" name, is a horse-trader. Owing to the stringency of the money market, he could not conduct one of those star elopements to any great

extent. So Mrs. Rasgorshek nailed her husband's watch and the money, to overcome the impossible. She shoved the booty down into her shoe and gave the alarm of a burglary to her liege lord when he awakened in the morning to find his valuables scattered over the floor—a scene that would have done honor to "Bill Sykes," or any other of the "profesh."

While her husband was at the station she gave Skeleton the purloined watch and $5, and promised to secure more of the wherewithal and meet him a little way out of town, call in a preacher and fly with the wings of love to the beautiful summer clime of Minneapolis. But burglaries are always more or less investigated, and Detective Savage described in vivid terms the awful fate in store for the man who would commit so great a crime. So when she was summoned before Captain Haze and that gentleman had talked to her in a kindly, fatherly way, she made the confession. It was thought that the man was in Pacific Junction, but there will probably be no attempt at arrest, as the "jig's up," and the watch may be peaceably returned. Mrs. Rasgorshek says she still loves Skeleton and would fly to him at once were it possible.

Evening World Herald 1896

Mrs. Ada Rasgorshek, aged 55 years, died Sunday morning at her home, 2908 North Twenty-sixth street, after an illness extending over a long period. She was the wife of Gabriel Rasgorshek, president of the Eagles, aerie No. 38. Mrs. Rasgorshek had lived in Omaha for thirty years. The funeral will be held Tuesday afternoon from the residence at 2 o'clock to the Sacred Heart church at 2:30 o'clock. Burial will be in Holy Sepulcher cemetery.

Evening World Herald 1916

Broken

Alfred and Jennie Trudeau

Drunkenness and divorce run deep in my family. Tales of one or another, or in this case both, are a common speckled thread. Trails of brokenness and dysfunction, blood-shot memories and traits passed on.

The Trudeau's, Alfred and Jennie, my 2nd great-grand-parents, were happy at one time, I expect. Young love led to a March wedding, and in August 1883 the birth of their son. A year later, my great-grandmother was born, followed by two more children. But by 1900, a divorce and Alfred left for Montana, to begin a new life. In 1901, the youngest son, Elmer, died at 14. A sad broken home remained.

Seeking alimony and with an ax to grind, in 1910, Mrs. Trudeau sued her ex-husband, so the newspaper story goes. Alfred, accused of financial skipping out and drunkenness, came into a family inheritance after his mother died a year ear-lier. Jennie wanted her share. A lawsuit built on bitterness, grief and resentment of her hard work keeping the family afloat. She believed she was owed payback for her angry and grief-stricken past.

Little is known about the children's family experience, or life thereafter. Ralph, the eldest remained living at home in Iowa, took care of his mom, and never married. A narrow and perhaps stunted life. Alice, lovingly known as Aunt Allie, the youngest came close, but also never married. She lived a full and success-ful life in Omaha. Grandpa was fond of his only aunt and drawn to her sweet disposition. In later years, he even named his horse after her.

And then there was Winifred, my great-grandmother. A middle child, the eldest daughter, also known as Winnie.

At 18, she married. A beautiful bride and bright light for her mom. She made an early escape with a friendly barber named Fred. A year later, their only child, a son was born — my later infamous grandpa.

Winifred was difficult and unlikeable, many in the family claimed. My grandpa moved to Los Angeles as a young man. Many of the Greenelsh clan had also made their way west, and his dad, Fred, and his mom Winifred soon followed. But as the

MRS. TRUDEAU WANTS HER PAY.

Divorced Husband Falls Heir to Small Fortune—Alimony Due.

Shenandoah, March 12.—Attorneys have brought suit for Mrs. Jennie E. Trudeau of Coin, against her former husband, A. F. Trudeau, to gain alimony acquired by the defendant since their divorce was granted in 1900. The plaintiff alleges that after she had obtained divorce on her charges of drunkenness and non-support and been given the custody of two of their four children, she has not been free from various troubles of which he was the source. That she has been compelled to pay large bills contracted by the defendant in her name; that she has kept a boarding house, and of late being in impaired health, she has been compelled to take to rough work to support the children he has decreed to support. That she has sent one child through college and paid the funeral expenses of one that died, while her divorced husband was drinking his pay away. Now the defendant, by the death of his father and mother, has fallen heir to an estate of $3,000, and Mrs. Trudeau thinks by dint of her deprivations and sacrificing labors she is entitled to $2,00 of it.

Jennie Trudeau Sues for Alimony

family rumor goes, dad and son kind of wished she had stayed behind.

To me, in my young and vague memories, Winifred, my great-grandma, was always old, quiet and dour. She wore ugly black oxford old lady shoes, her hose in little piles of wrinkles around her ankles. Like all of them, doing the best she could.

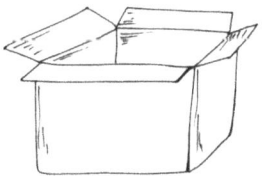

The Patriarch

James and Elizabeth Greenelsh

James Greenelsh was a good talker, a skill he refined in early years as a debater with a literary society. And no doubt a well-connected, well-liked character, but with a drinking problem—and perhaps a little inside pool hall leverage.

I never heard much about the Greenelsh patriarch, my great-great-grandfather and yet there was plenty that could have leaked out of the guarded silo of family secrets, conveniently left back in Burlington Junction, Missouri, lost in history and locked in family memories. Most of the flock of seven surviving children born to James and Elizabeth Greenelsh, eventually migrated to California. The elders stayed behind, as did one son.

James Lewis Greenelsh's early years in Ohio had to be difficult. His mother and both of his siblings died when he was five years old, around 1860, leaving him and his dad behind. In

Pool Hall

1863, his dad remarried a woman named Rebecca, whose first husband died in the Civil War; she came with four children. Years later, in 1876, James married one of his stepsisters, Elizabeth Davis.

James' dad left him well off, with a farm, though James was not the farming type. He sold or lost it and moved the family to Burlington Junction, Missouri in 1892. He then purchased a pool hall and livery stable; the beginning of his wayward ways, now a father in his mid-30s with a wife and eight children.

In 1893, his first known arrest — forging a $150 note. Our patriarch became a familiar face in the Marysville and Burlington Junction courts — a repeat and notorious offender in bootlegging and gaming aspects of his pool hall business. His most infamous, (being one of the oldest and the most frequent violators of the Missouri liquor laws), 30 counts and a historic sentence — 15 years in jail, in 1907.

Grizzled and gutsy, he talked his way out, for an early parole. "Your honor I don't want anything but justice and as little of that as possible," he addressed the court on one occasion. He bargained, offering to get out of the pool hall business and be good, if he was paroled. Serving less than a year — his deal worked, once he could pay his fine, and understand the judge's warning not to reengage in such business again, or his parole would be revoked.

He later wrote the judge claiming that he was not able to find any other work he could do and intended to get back into the pool hall business. His old persuasive antics kicked in again, offering to be a place to *reform* his class of customers — if he could do things his way, causing another good laugh in his proverbial court-room visit. Conveniently, the judge dismissed James of parole in 26 of the charges.

Meanwhile, his wife took in laundry and sewing and did other side jobs to help support their large family.

James Lewis Greenelsh died in 1930 at age 76, working until the end. Profession: Tax Assessor—a position he held for eight years, elected for four consecutive terms. Neither his obituary nor family recollections noted his notorious past. But it was known that he "always ate Post Toasties and oatmeal, and always put vinegar on his chocolate cake."

Nodaway Circuit Court.

Nodaway county's grand jury brought in one hundred and ten indictments last week and created some uneasiness among those brethren who usually find it convenient to visit in Blanchard, Clarinda and other neighbor towns just across the Iowa line. One of our exchanges from Maryville says that Judge Ellison came down on the booze peddlers in a way that jarred them "clear down in their boots." James Greenelsh, an old offender, plead guilty to twenty-nine courts, was promptly fined $300 and given six months in jail on each court—but escaped his total jail sentence of more than fourteen years by paying the $300 and being paroled, after an admonition to steer close to the straight and narrow path.

The Atchison County Mail 1908

James Greenelsh. veteran pool hall proprietor and notorious in court circles, was discharged from parole in 26 of the thirty cases against him for the illegal sale of liquor. He is still under parole in four cases.

Weekly Democrat Forum and Maryville Tribune 1909

GREENELSH A REFORMER

AGED OFFENDER TELLS COURT HE COULD REFORM CUSTOMERS

James Greenelsh, who has been in court more times than the oldest court house reporter can remember, stood before Judge Ellison again Monday afternoon while the judge who had sentenced him to fourteen years in the county jail examined his record under a recently granted parole.

"Let's see," said the judge, "you were kind enough to write me recently that you were going back into the pool hall business. I was sorry to hear it, too," continued the judge. "Couldn't you have found some other business?"

"I couldn't find anything else to do," replied the aged court attendant, and he favored the court with the same winning smile that he wore when the judge gave him the most severe sentence ever handed out to an offender of the state's liquor laws.

"What class of customers have you?" asked the court in referring to the business in which Greenelsh has been engaged in during the major portion of his court career.

"Well, I could reform some of them if I had my way," replied the grizzled offender and the court and spectators joined in a general laugh.

Greenelsh was paroled at the last term of court on thirty cases for violations of the liquor laws. Prosecuting Attorney Wiles stated that he had received no complaint from Burlington Junction people and Judge Ellison dismissed Greenelsh from parole in 26 of the cases. The aged man will still remain under parole, however, as there are four cases on the docket. He will have to appear again at the November term of court.

Daily Democrat Forum 1909

The Barber
with the Long Neck

Great-grandfather Fred Greenelsh

The story is short, as is the span of my knowledge. My great-grandfather **Fred Greenelsh**, one of seven surviving children, inherited the better traits of his father, a gregarious man. Cutting hair and shaving chins, Fred chatted with the men of Burlington Junction, MO. unlike his dad who chattered his way out of bootlegging charges.

Fred, along with his difficult wife Winifred, moved out to California in 1923, to join their only son. An early pioneer of Van Nuys, CA., they built a home. Active with church, the church choir and the Masonic lodge (gathering places for this sociable man), he was also a barber — with a very long neck.

Some say a long neck suggests one is wise, elegant and poised or empathetic and compassionate. Some say one is an intellectual with an independent streak. Could Fred be any or all of these? I'll never know. But I do know he seemed to be a kind man — with a very long neck.

Fred Greenelsh died June 8, 1951.

He was 67 years old.

Fred's Barber License

Fred Greenelsh with Infant – My Uncle John in the Background

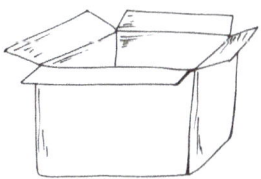

The May Company Box

The May Company Box

I scan over more boxes arranged on the floor. I settle on an old May Company department store gift box, located in one of the larger boxes of Grandma and Grandpa's stuff. The top tattered and taped, May Company's classic box design—a collection of drawings of Los Angeles landmarks: City Hall, the Griffith Observatory, UCLA's Royce Hall, the Music Center, and the oil rigs that line the LA harbor.

I sit on my silk blue meditation cushion with my afternoon jasmine green tea at my side. As usual, it appears to be another mixed collection of pictures and papers, with some loose Kodak slides strewn on top. I first open an envelope addressed to Ethelyn Rasgorshek Greenelsh. Grandma's 50th high school reunion booklet mailed to her in 1976, Van Nuys High School, class of 1926. It was their first time to have a class reunion and couples were pictured together in a mini yearbook. My grandmother looks happy, but they all look so old!

I'm curious about the slides, but don't have a slide projector on hand, so I hold them up to the light in the window. They are color images, from the late 1960s. I see a familiar grouping of my brothers with me in front of a car, of course. The other photos are also family groupings, probably taken at one of the Greenelsh family summer reunions held at Cuesta Park in San Luis Obispo.

Under the slides, I find a stack of photos, some quite old of my grandfather as a child, my great-grandmother and her mom, my dad as a baby, and an old Model T car with a dog looking out the window.

At the bottom, I find a large envelope and see the note made from a red marking pen. It's a collection of my grandfather's career and retirement party memories from the Southern California Gas Company. His old identification card from 1941 looks like a mug shot. He was 37, 5'6" and weighed just 145 lbs. I didn't realize he was that small in his prime years. Grandma was only 5'3", like me.

Grandfather's Southern California Gas Company I.D. Card

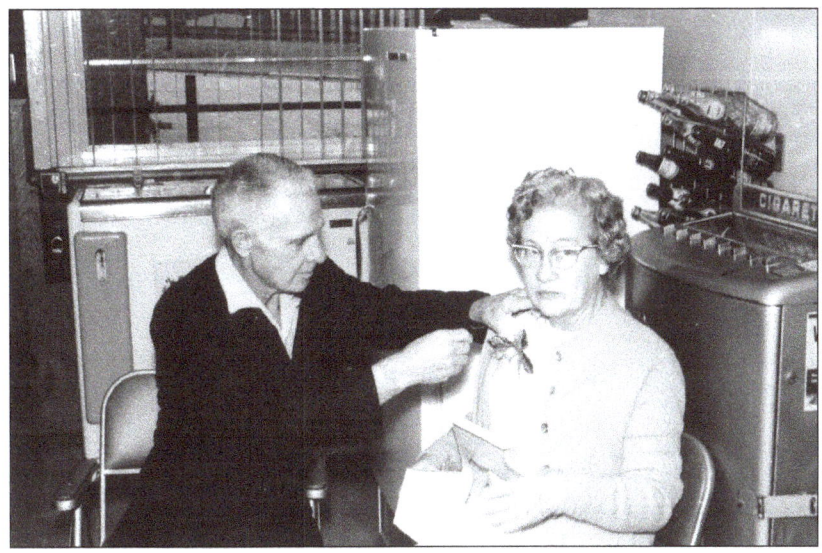

Grandpa and Grandma

Overall, his collection pretty much makes sense—except for the Oregon City Municipal Elevator Lifetime Pass issued to my grandfather for some reason. His retirement party pictures remind me of mine—a cake in a conference room and obligatory smiles—except for my grandmother, who didn't seem keen on the gifted corsage for "the wife".

I come to the end of what's offered here. A yellowed, folded piece of tissue paper, that no doubt came with the gift box, sits at the bottom, ready to protect these contents again—until the next time someone opens the May Company Box.

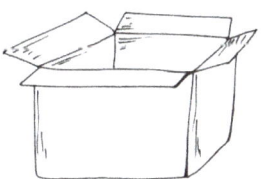

The Blatz Box and Box #2

The Blatz Box

The box alone is at least 63 yrs. old. Pabst Blue Ribbon stopped producing Blatz beer in 1959, coincidently the same year of my birth. It originally contained four, 6-bottle cartons of Blatz, Milwaukee's Finest Beer. Old scotch and other packing tape hang off the tattered corrugated edges and hold together a tear in one corner of the old dusty brown cardboard box, probably once discarded in the back of a local grocery or liquor store, free for the taking. Now, in a thick blue ink marker, *Pictures and Bibles* written on several sides, hint of its contents.

The dust makes me sneeze, as I enter a familiar, yet unfamiliar world, a collection of related and random items. It contains mostly the Greenelsh side of the family photos — and miscellaneous items from my grandparents and great-grand-parents. The first layer is the cover made from the Classified Section of the paper, 1950. I don't think it's meaningful, other than protecting the contents, but you never know. Other news-papers from Omaha, 1932. I presume there is an article that meant something to great-aunt Allie. She was the only one, on the Greenelsh side, living there at the time.

An assortment of photos stare up at me, the big formal old studio black and white portraits, as well as small snapshots from various family gatherings, trips and picnics, and old photo post-cards popular back then. Some look like they were from my great-grandparents' era, per my assessment of fashion and photo type and quality. With magnifying glass in hand, I look for clues. So many don't have any notes, some have one person I recognize and occasionally I score a find, a new piece to the family puzzle. I want to jump into the family setting and say "Hey, it's me, Mary

Ann, your great or great-great-granddaughter. So happy to meet you." And of course, ask so many questions, study their appearance, voices and mannerisms. All the things I can't get, but only imagine from this careful dig in the Blatz Box.

Randomly, the excavation finds my grandpa's high school yearbooks. I poke around and see that he was the Senior class president in his round wire rim glasses, so cool for 1923. His nickname was "Greenie". It seemed to be a thing for all the male seniors to have a frat-boy-like name. He was a rather serious type and member of the Literary Club. None of this seems much like the grandpa I knew. I also find programs, in later years of those important dinners with the Southern California Gas Company when he was honored for his 30 years of work, and 40 years, then retirement. There are my great-grandparents' hymnals, my uncle's graduation announcements, newspaper clippings of my dad's tour with his college dance band, where he played the saxophone, and an obituary of my great-great-grandmother. There are a couple of old toys, a small dusty towel or diaper and an old unopened pair of rust colored dress shoelaces. There's a 1940 Contract Bridge book with a congratulations inscribed to my great-grandmother. And a 1950 booklet titled "Survival Under Atomic Attack", distributed by the Office of Civil Defense, State of California, Earl Warren, Governor. And a leather pouch holds a never-been-used arm band issued to my grandfather, by the Southern California Gas Company as a part of an Emergency Repair Corp. Serial number 3452, accompanied with an Oath of Allegiance to the US constitution, required by the Office of Civilian Defense. I'm assuming this was issued during WW2.

Box #2

There's another box I call Box #2 from my grandparents. It originally contained some sort of primer paint cans, now another assortment of pictures and various memories from the Greenelsh side of the family. Again, with blue ink marker noting its contents, and old newspaper topping that within. The scrappy edges, old tape and torn corners contain more stories and stuff.

My grandparents, both sets, on Dad's side of the family (Greenelsh and Rasgorshek), were members of fraternal groups like the Masons, Eastern Star, Rebekah. My dad continued that tradition as a member of the Elks club. Odd stuff I can't relate to, but important to them and their heritage. So, this box starts with something that looks like a large white fabric envelope, with satin trim and cord with tassels. A presentation piece, per its blue stamped San Fernando Lodge information, indicating that "Bro", my grandfather Leo Paul Greenelsh, entered, passed and was raised from May 1945 to Oct 1945. Something honorary. Something I don't get. Similarly, I didn't get some of the old traditions at my dad's memorial either, held at an Elks Lodge. The "Bro" was honored with white men in robes.

I find a file of my grandfather's conflict with the Southern Pacific Railroad. He owned a ranch in Newhall, which one had to cross over the railroad to enter. He had to maintain the crossing but was having issues with the railroad and dirt bike riders who had been causing damage. He wrote in a letter that he wanted responsibility transferred, so he could more easily sell his property. As he was retired, he wanted to downsize and have the income from the sale, without concern and liability issues over the crossing. I remember Grandpa always being upset about this, but have fond memories of watching trains, waving to the caboose driver and flattening pennies on the tracks.

I also find closed savings account bank books. One is a joint account between Grandpa's mom, Grandma Greenelsh (Winifred) and my **aunt Bonnie**, his daughter with his first wife. The other bank account book is between Grandpa and his mom. There was always a heavy issue hanging over Grandpa and Bonnie, with whom he was estranged, over an issue with money between his mom, Grandma Greenelsh, and Bonnie. I'm wondering if these two bank books shed any light on that story.

Grandma Greenelsh was a widow. In later years, Bonnie shared that she had such fondness for her Grandpa Fred Greenelsh but wasn't fond of Grandma Greenelsh (as others also seemed to feel). I don't know the story about money taken, presumably, by Bonnie, out of the joint account. But I can see where Grandpa, perhaps not knowing of the joint account between his mother and daughter, had some concern. It was a lot of money back then. Did Bonnie take advantage of her grandmother who she wasn't fond of? Did she have permission to use the money, or did Grandma Greenelsh use the money? In any case, it caused a riff that was never healed before any of them died.

Sadly, the last time I saw Grandpa, just a week before he passed away, he called me Bonnie. Thanks to my dad's urging, I got to know Bonnie myself when I lived and worked near where she was living up in the San Francisco Bay Area. I was managing a travel agency at the time and Bonnie had been a travel agent too, so we had some common ground. Her wounds were deep with Grandpa. I was only in my twenties and didn't have any perspective about family history. It was sad. She was a nice lady. They both were hurt.

I also discover photos of **Aunt Allie**, great-aunt Alice — great-grandma Greenelsh's sister who lived in Omaha. Grandpa was always very fond of her and looked after her in her older years. She never married or had children. She was treasured, a sweet and warm soul in my grandpa's view. Her photos tell a story I have yet to put together.

Next, I come upon Grandpa's old license from the Department of Agriculture for "Paul's Poultry". He raised turkeys in

Newhall. As kids, my dad and uncle did not care for working there and never ate poultry or eggs.

There are also old escrow papers for the great-grandparent's Van Nuys Friar Street house and cemetery plot purchases. Most interesting is a letter great-grandpa (Fred) Greenelsh sent to a friend postmarked June 5, 1951 packed along with his death certificate and his 1950–51 Barber's License. He died June 8, 1951, just three days later. His friend must have given the letter back to Grandma Greenelsh understanding that it was probably his last thing he had written.

I also have great-grandma Greenelsh's wallet with her driver's license when she was 70 years old (5'4" and 129 lbs.) along with her Eastern Star Lodge cards and some credit cards. And her empty key holder with a framed lucky charm penny. Grandpa's 1922 yearbook from Burlington Junction High School, missing from the Blatz box collection, is in here. Known as a very busy bee, he was the class secretary. In addition, I find a couple of books given to Grandpa in high school, *Burke's Speech* and *Heavenward Way*. They were both given to him on May 9, 1923, I expect maybe for a graduation.

In both boxes, I find random pictures of me and my brothers. School pictures sent, no doubt in an annual Christmas card, and then retained in some box or drawer of collected family photos, once treasured by someone who felt, for a moment, remembered.

I tuck everything back, neatly until we meet again. Who knows what will become of all these old treasures, stuff, minutia. These lives and memories once treasured.

Oh Grandpa

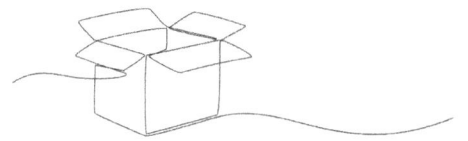

Grandpa's Albums

Grandpa's Albums

It started when I opened an orange photo album—a picture of Ronald Reagan and a random clipping of a child from a magazine ad. The rest empty pages. Since then, I've been avoiding this box of photo albums, just as I avoid the subject of Grandpa. A recent revisit of the box, followed by an angst-ridden nightmare, I realize it may be time for me to explore Grandpa's inner sanctum of oddities.

The fifteen albums (late 1970s–early 1980s) are held together with the sticky pages and a sheet of clear plastic that pulls away, so photos stay in place. Cheap old drug-store-purchased, exterior covers with puppies, flowers, nature scenes or young couples frolicking on beaches. Inside the now unsticking pages, I find a possible roadmap of Grandpa's mind, a random semi-organized collection of pictures, news clippings and other items he accumulated, now waiting for me. I enter Grandpa's world, one weird album and reflective (but troubling) hour at a time.

Some photos are arranged in logical groupings: old black and whites of Grandpa's childhood days; and various ones in color I remember—family reunions, weddings, school pictures, summer visits, the old house, his horse named Allie and his dog named Sam, and one of me fashioning an unfortunate new perm. Less logical disbursements: Ronald Reagan, Ronald and Nancy Reagan, Ronald Reagan and George Bush; a covered bridge, my senior prom, Dad's remarriage, more relatives, and Gerald and Betty Ford. And other pictures that don't make sense—or maybe they do. I find questionable photos clipped from magazines or advertisements, like the one I first saw in the orange album, scattered here and there.

Obituaries and funeral notices are placed throughout the albums, everyone Grandma and Grandpa knew or admired such as the local librarian and local the newspaper editor; a cherished family member, Uncle Jimmy, per The Elks Yell, an Exalted Ruler from 1931–32; and Grandpa's beloved Aunt Allie remembrances unrelated to Jimmy.

And articles — so many articles! Like the stack of junk kept in piles on desks, or in cabinet files, from Newhall, LA, Burlington Junction and Omaha newspapers, The Freemason and Gas Company News publications; and various others that come in junk mail. Clippings memorializing the old days of his Newhall community and Midwest hometown, the old baseball club, a train depot closing, a circus or new stop sign in town. And miscellany, a lot of it: Saccharine vs. Marijuana, the latest in cataract surgery, an Omaha born clarinetist performing at a local art college, his cousin's 50th wedding anniversary story — the list goes on.

Clearly, an early *Make America Great Again* sympathizer, Grandpa kept articles of a familiar theme in his version of scrapbooking. Articles include the dangers of marijuana and drug reform; the stupidity of the Child and Welfare Act; debates on alcoholism not being a disease; the benefits of one-room child schooling of the past; a Freemason article, *The Energy Shortage Myth*; William F. Buckley, Jr., on an amendment to curb the Supreme Court; and another Freemason article on the true meaning of America's forgotten pyramid symbol on the dollar bill. Of course, there are also various unflattering articles of Governor Jerry Brown and President Jimmy Carter. Grandpa's collection of topics, a scorecard to have on the ready for any hint of a left-leaning discussion at the dinner table or the reason why the good old days slipped away — all the subjects we avoided around Grandpa.

The random, bric-a-brac of sprinkled memories, empty pages and odd junk, the stack of unfiltered stuff, stuck on sticky pages weave around unrelated pictures and articles: A Magic Mountain family picnic night ticket; an article on referral services for dentists; a racist joke involving Santa Claus, business cards for horseshoeing services; my first business card — a young travel agent with Matador Travel; a poem, "Challenges for the True Mason"; another poem and picture of a dog named Harry; programs for high school graduations; and a list of government representatives in 1979.

The photo album exploration and random list goes on, some other interesting historical articles and tidbits. Grandpa's soapbox of societal concerns and politics were typical of him — we were used to that.

But the inclusion of several photos of attractive young children placed throughout the albums reveal disturbing clues to Grandpa's mind — strange stuff and shit I just don't get.

———

Meet Tara, a cute almost suggestive picture from an insurance company ad campaign, glued on an inside cover. On the outside cover is a picture of a happy young couple gazing at each other surrounded by nature. Tara is **maybe 5 years old**.

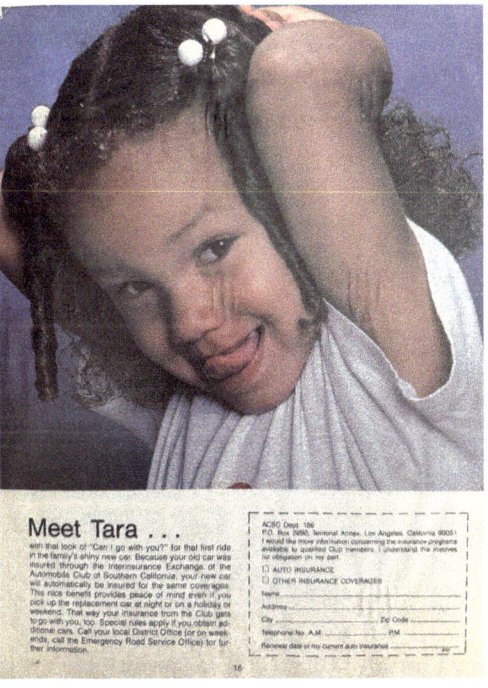

Meet Tara . . .

Meet Kim, a young girl with braces, **maybe 11 years old**, mid-photo album and, another full-size ad. On this red album cover, a picture of puppies arranged on a blanket.

Meet Kim

Meet Katy, she continues a disturbing series of ads from the auto club encouraging membership — a cute, freckled-face young girl, **pre-teen**. She's located on the inside cover of another album with a cute dog and puppies, this time playful on green grass.

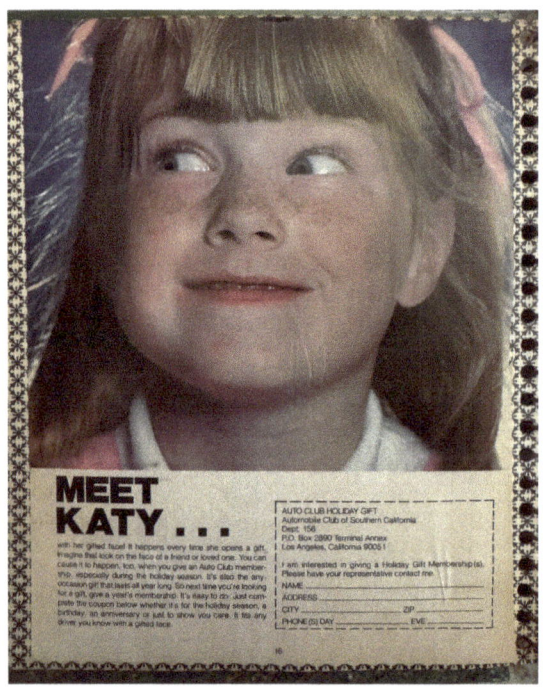

Meet Annie, a cute toddler, **maybe just three years old.** She's in the album, with the cover of young boys goofing around.

MEET
ANNIE

Meet Andrew James, he's **maybe six**. Pick any album cover — the pink daisies, a waterfall scene, an old-world map — or the orange one.

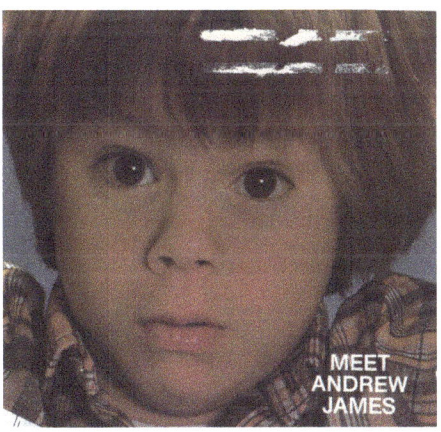

MEET
ANDREW
JAMES

Exploring the contents of Grandpa's photo albums mirrors my memories of him. But his criminal behavior revealed in later years created an unsettling blend of thoughts and emotions for the whole family.

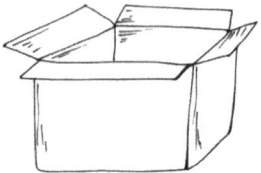

Grandpa Visit

The last semi-sane visit with Grandpa, he lured me to lunch and an ask to see him. He had family items I might want to peruse, or maybe take before — before who knows what.

Grandma was in hospice, and Grandpa was in trouble, laying low, after the first arrest. In a trailer back in Newhall, Grandpa sorted out the leftovers of their lives before their respective next chapters began.

Curious about mysteries kept in taped up boxes, stored in the back of closets or on dusty garage shelves — unburied treasures from the past, far-off places, a fantasy of hidden family grandeur in ordinary brown cardboard boxes, I headed up north, about 30 miles to Newhall.

Grandpa sat waiting with his twitching jowls, each twitch counting time, on his twisted Dali internal clock. He was always on time, always early. The rest, always late. Displayed on a kitchen dining room table were at best 10 random things: a green ceramic vase, Tupperware, a plastic container for dentures. In his sane mind, maybe something I would want. In my semi-sane expectations, an unfulfilled and sad truth about what had become of their lives. I took the vase and two old drinking glasses he pushed on me.

Lunch at a still normal, brand name, nearby coffee shop, Denny's or the like—as always, good enough. Grandpa, rigid, always about the rules, but now his life was like an antique broken wind-up toy, aimlessly living in a once loved past. His mixed-up motions, rules be damned, and my taped up and stored away emotions. His, you can have dessert after you eat your meal, now childlike—a chocolate milkshake and fries. We ate. No judgement. That would come soon enough.

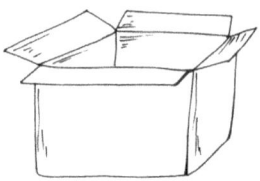

Like Fog

Clouds and Fog

The second to the last time I saw Grandpa, like much of his life is one of those muddled memories. A few days before Christmas, 1988. Grandpa, released from the Men's Colony in San Luis Obispo, after five years. At one time the oldest prisoner in the State of California, a free, but unwanted man. At 84, aged and feeble.

His new home, an old downtown Ventura hotel, his only option. I stopped to check in on him on my drive up the coast and leave a Christmas gift—a new shirt. The dark, musty and dreary room resembled the state of his last years. My numbness kept me connected and disconnected to the reality of his life and crime. I still cared for the smelly, empty and homeless looking man.

At a recent David Gray concert, a simple lyric, say hello and wave goodbye, reminded me of those memories that come and leave with little imprint, as opposed to those memories that roll in like a thick fog and immerse, surround, and settle in. I prefer the former. But, when invited or uninvited, Grandpa's fog bank, hanging just off my emotional coast, came to stay awhile, like the June Gloom, or May Gray.

Childhood memories come and go, happy, normal times like riding Grandpa's horse; driving the tractor up the steep driveway; flattening pennies on the train tracks; or waiting for trains to go by at night, as I tried to sleep. The whooshing of the sleek passenger trains and the rumble of the freight cars I counted instead of sheep. The horse auctions down the street at Randall's Ranch on a Saturday night or a walk to A & W on hot summer days for a well-earned root beer float. And getting Silly Putty stuck on the back seat of his car.

In contrast, heavy laden later memories linger like visits to Grandpa in Camarillo State Hospital—a pit stop for a problematic pedophile or in prison sitting in the courtyard making uncomfortable small talk. Visits to Grandma in hospice wondering what she knew and knowing she would never see him again, though married since 1935. Her funeral, him escorted by a sheriff to attend, sitting next to me holding my hand, sobbing, uncontrollably. I couldn't let myself cry, as if a shared moment condoned his decisions. Suspicious of his tears. Scared of mine. Sad for Grandma.

My urged last visit, several weeks later, January 29, 1989, my 30th birthday. I remember two things: for some unknown reason, the awful 80s pink knit outfit I wore; and Grandpa thinking I was Bonnie, his daughter he had not talked to for so many years. He was an unhealed man, gravely ill in the Ventura County Hospital, surrounded by no one. He died alone, February 11, just two days after his 85th birthday. His small funeral, uneventful— barely memorable.

Like the fog of life and war, it's confusing and complicated— the memories, fractured relationships, and chaotic feelings. Every time I revisit, the emotions, the mess, there is a letting go, a clearing resonated in another recent, reembraced lyric.

Love is the opening door . . .
—Elton John (Tumbleweed Connection)

More Women's Voices

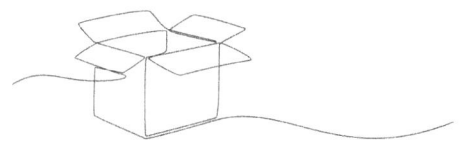

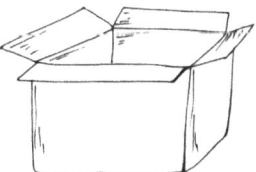

Desires Out of Reach

Winifred Greenelsh

In this photo, my **great-grandmother Greenelsh, Winifred** looks at the camera as if she were posing for Andrew Wyeth. Confident or perhaps a little irritated, the desolate landscape her canvas, during a long journey from Missouri to California. A husband and son's desire to live out west, her desires possibly left behind. Her feminine and confrontational expression front and center, perhaps a message regarding her life in flux.

In my mom's early years and certainly for most women prior, women's life transitions were rarely of their choosing. Choices, if offered, were limited. Mom had dreams of becoming a commercial artist. Even though she was voted the most artistic in her high school, for a vocation she could choose secretarial, nursing or beauty school. Pick one. Art wasn't one. Later, in her stay-at-home-mom years, she took art classes and painted here and there, but lacked confidence in her work. Her internal spark left to a simmer.

My mother was a fan of Andrew Wyeth's work and one summer, there was an exhibition of his paintings in San Francisco. When we took my brother David to a special clinic in the city, for his feet, Mom requested we also go to the exhibit. Her once-in-her-lifetime chance to see and reconnect with her artistic flame. The idea wasn't a big hit with the rest of us — nothing more boring than following Mom around in a museum. But we were all on board, even Dad's razor thin patience.

Dad looked and looked for parking in Balboa Park, with many little backseat helpers. Patience running out all around, hope was fading for Mom's one chance. She finally succumbed to Dad's claim that there was absolutely no parking to be found. Nothing could be done; it wasn't going to happen. She deflated. Dad exhaled. Kids relieved. We all missed an enriching opportunity.

Mom related to Wyeth's most famous painting, Christina's World. The theme reinforced at different times in Mom's life I expect—not getting what she wanted. Her internal desires, like great-grandmother Winifred's, out of reach.

Christina's World by Andrew Wyeth (1948)

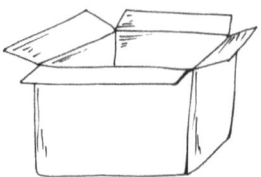

Powdery Women

Grandmothers Lulu and Ethelyn

The look: soft short white or grey hair with a permanent, glasses, pearls or a pearl drop necklace, and perfectly soft powdered skin—wearing a housedress, or flowered number for church or a women's group. Grandmotherly and comforting. This uniform style is found throughout my boxes of photographs. It's safe and conforming. Both of my grandmothers, **Lulu**, and **Ethelyn** fit the mold of powdery women.

They were also strong and beautiful but appeared gentle, loving, good mothers and grandmothers. This was their limited and accepted look for the time, reminding us of their role and place.

Lulu with Family or Friends

I like to look at this photo, whenever I see it in the stack — it shows up in a couple of my boxes. I stop and chuckle. Lulu is the 3rd from the left. I don't know who the other women are, probably some family relations. They aren't the classic powdery woman. Bold, no façade, hair and pearls be damned — but always carrying a purse.

Grandma Ethelyn (l) and Me (r)

Grandma Ethelyn and I were close and alike in many ways. Both 5'3", we wore the same shoe size and shared similar interests. In her younger years, she had a lot of pizzaz — playing saxophone and looking like a flapper girl. As she became older, she worried, talked of health concerns, and embraced the powdery woman persona. We looked alike in our younger years, but I refuse to become an old lady. I donned a white powdery prom dress in 1977, but that's a far as I go!

Rocks and Rebels

My Drawings and Rocks

Sprinkled throughout the family are the rock-solid women. Sturdy and stable, the glamourless glue who held the family together; they quietly kept everyday life in order. Busy being the backbone, their stories didn't usually make family headlines.

My grandmother **Lulu York O'Neil** was one rock. Though her earlier years met the rebel label, being divorced shortly after her first son was born, in 1899. She remarried in 1906 — an interfaith marriage seemingly accepted in the not very religious York clan, and unknown to the O'Neill's back in Ireland.

Married life to her Irish lad Timothy was filled with family and four more children. She led the life of a farmer's wife. Days were filled with chores and more chores. She tended to children, fed the farm hands and menfolk at the mid-day supper, and took care of the house, supplies, meals and neighbors. She repaired every seam that needed sewing, canned, preserved, and saw that kids got grown. Occasionally she made time for church, a picnic or family gathering. She found joy in her rose garden and the love of all in her life. But she became a widow too soon, in 1935, and acquired the burden that came with 40 acres and a new husbandless life.

Lulu's mom, my great-grandmother, was another reliable rock. Like her daughter, **Huldah Matthews York**, she also had her early rebel years. Known as a spunky lady, she divorced (1870-1874) after leaving her irresponsible fire and brimstone, meaner-than-a-snake, itinerant preacher husband. With two surviving children and ailing parents in tow, she came west on an immigrant train from Indiana to California where her brother had already made his home. She later met and married Andrew

York, fifteen years her senior with five children. They had two more children and settled into their large, merged family life. She took interest in the healing properties of plants and herbs and became known as the mid-wife of the rural Templeton hills. Putting off her own need for surgery, until it was too late, she died in 1916 at 68.

My great-grandmother **Ethel Rasgorshek** was a rock on the other side of the family. Rebel tendencies skipped her completely. Her mom died when she was just 19. She married just a few years later in 1902, to a rock-solid man, with weak lungs. They moved west for his health and settled into a 2 ½ acre homestead in the new San Fernando Valley region in Los Angeles. It was a happy but hardworking life centered around extended family, a poultry ranch, summer treks to the Inland Empire to pick fruit, holding recitals at her home with her daughter playing saxophone and son on the piano, and being the wife of the High Priest of the Van Nuys Royal Arch Masons.

Her daughter, **Ethelyn**, my grandmother, made up for her mom's lack of rebel ways. Grandma married three times before she was 30. She played her saxophone in an all-female jazz band. And, I'd like to think had a great time before her rock years. She ultimately settled into motherhood and the life of a dutiful wife and raising responsible boys.

My mom was born a rebel at heart. A surprise baby to Lulu and Timothy O'Neil, she arrived on, and disrupted Christmas Eve. Mom marched to a different and artistic drum. After settling for beauty school, she left her rural roots, with a man and a mysterious decade to follow.

Marriage found her four times, her last to a man 14 years younger — my dad. She was a good mom and loved her family — and divorced again. The 1960s spoke to her rebellious desires, her love of nature and an artistic way. But she muted her inner rebel for the life of a rock-solid single mom.

These strong women and numerous aunts were my female foundation. Their tenacity, courage, sacrifice, and ambition gave me a solid core. Their rebellious DNA flows through my blood — it gives me oxygen and an open door. Their stories are a part of mine — but I divorced just one time.

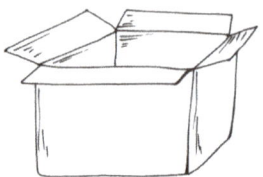

The Importance of Aunts

Aunts

The sisterhood of the aunts was an important force in my life. Only one is left, **Aunt Gloria**. The uncles are all gone now. I was also fond of them, though some sit more on the sidelines of my memory bank. But the aunts I watched and listened to passed on important tidbits and insights. Gloria still does.

The aunts were the lighter source of wisdom and connection. They were the ones who coordinated and made fun gatherings happen; the glue that held traditions and relations together, holders of stories, knowledge, and recipes. They remembered those who came before and how they died. They warned of our vulnerabilities, what tendencies ran in the family and watched over us all.

Auntie Hi, shared her knowledge and love of rocks. She spearheaded family rock-hounding adventures. **Aunt Marguerite** showed me how to make a lizard snare out of long grass. We'd watch for them to peek their heads out of a big pile of rocks in her front yard and snare them — great fun for us, not so much for the lizards. **Aunt Jean** liked pretty things, girly lunches and made me a new Easter dress. **Sharon** was always so sweet, and Gloria inspired my view of life outside a small town, a love for travel and old family photos. Auntie Hi, Aunt Jean and Gloria were teachers, and probably the first women in the family with four-year college degrees.

I don't remember any great-aunts but do remember four great-great-aunts. They had a serious number of wrinkles, smiles, and an abundance of sweetness. **Aunt May** wore numerous silver bracelets that dangled up and down her weathered arms. They intrigued me. It was fun to see **Aunt Margaret**. She had (reportedly) over 1400 salt and pepper shakers and displayed them in glass cabinets throughout her house. She also saved egg cartons, strawberry baskets and even string that was wrapped around roasts, in perfect stacks. We would go to see **Aunt Susie** on Sunday drives. Her room at the old folks home smelled of cigars once smoked by Uncle Otto. Lighthearted, and ready to marry again, she became engaged in her 90s. And beloved **Aunt Allie**, I only met once, but Grandpa spoke fondly of her often. Her collection of photos live in the Greenelsh box—unattached to remembered stories. She never married but was engaged to a WW1 soldier who didn't make it home.

I add myself to the list of aunts, a great-aunt and perhaps someday will add another great to my title. I am a holder of family stories, maybe important tidbits and more than a few recipes. I wonder how I will be remembered. The collection of wrinkles is growing.

Gleaning, Resilience, and Synchronicity

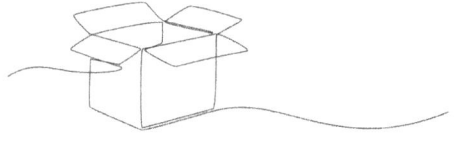

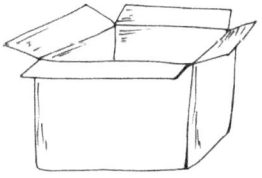

Fifth Date

My Drawing of Daniel

The first few dates, our best attire, wrinkle free. Large bags checked in, no carry on, no weight, no worry. We shared only the best, the accomplishments, the grand journeys and impressive tales, sprinkled with carefully crafted bits and pieces of our respective pasts.

Attraction, with a safe place to unpack, started to grow. Having been down the dating, winding road before, with brake lights on, we navigated personal histories; a collection of mismatched bags, or perhaps a whole set of luggage. The weight of life, life choices and circumstances. Those we packed with our best-then selves, and those left on our emotional doorsteps. The stories spanning our up to mid-life years, we parsed slowly — in control.

It was the fifth date. I cooked my first dinner for Daniel — *Bon Appetit*-worthy, of course! Around the white Sears-purchased stove in my tiny postwar, wishful bungalow house, we cautiously unbuckled, unzipped, revealed, exposed. Easy and light, we unwrapped our neat secured stories. A playful competition began.

"Whose family is most dysfunctional?" We brought in the luggage, stirred the tomato red pasta sauce, and sipped on artisan ginger ales. Daniel took his cue.

"I grew up in a broken home. Parents were divorced, both remarried — Dad a couple of times."

"I did too. Dad remarried. Mom did not. It was her fourth marriage."

"I have four siblings — one step, two halves and a whole."

"I do too — three halves and one whole!"

"One of my sisters is an alcoholic."

"Yeah, my older brother too. It's that Irish in us."

"Irish here too. So, how long were you married?"

"Almost four years, before we divorced. No kids. But, as you know, I have a cat. You?"

"As you know, I'm a widower. My wife died — from alcoholism. I have a few kids, also a cat."

"I'm so sorry. I know you have two boys. You, you have others?"

"Yes."

"And?"

"I have another boy. He lives with his mom. She's a yoga teacher."

"Good to know." (He's starting to win.)

"What else you got?"

"Hmm. My uncle was raised by his grandparents, thinking they were his parents, and his mom, my grandmother, was his sister." (That's pretty good!)

"Ok, let's see here. My grandfather didn't know who his father was, or if his brother had the same father. By the way, my grandfather was a pioneer of early radio and TV for NBC!"

"Impressive. My grandfather was rather impressive himself." ('Am I really going there?')

"How so?"

"Well — my grandfather was a child molester — a convicted pedophile. The oldest prisoner in the State of California prison system! Beat that! Or maybe don't."

Silence.

"Yup—I have no more cards to play. You win!"

We laughed, feasted on pasta, and talked for hours. No one ran for the emergency exits. Brake lights off and bags fully unpacked. We both won that night. We got each other, and a sixth date—for life.

Gleaning

Me and Daniel
1970s

Every time I walk past the photos placed in a double frame in our bedroom, it reminds me of how many years have passed. The 1970s — just yesterday! Gleaned memories are still fresh, as is a more recent humbling conversation with our granddaughter.

"Who's that?"

"It's Grandpa. Can't you tell?"

"No! That's Grandpa?" she exclaims in disbelief.

As she continues to peruse the two photos, she looks at mine, then me.

"Nana, you used to be so pretty."

I sigh.

I still do when I look at that photo of my teenage self — sun-glassed, tank-topped and waist length sun-bleached golden-brown hair, pulled back in a red cowboy scarf, proudly displaying a just-picked bunch of grapes. My husband's photo sits side by side, same vintage — tan, shirtless, pukka shell beads and good-boy long hair on the beach, Diamond Head in the background. It would be years later when we would meet, even though these snapshots were probably taken almost the same time in 1975.

Over our ritual morning coffee and tea, my husband and I sit outside watching the birds on the fountain — their youthful greeting dance of the day — and our best conversations, with and without the assist from the day's first glance at CNN, the stock market and endless email.

"I saw you checking out that 70s photo again when you got up. So, what do you remember about that actual day?" I ask, trying to glean new insights to my husband's past and his philosophical present.

"Hmm, I think I had just been told that the track program (why I went to the University of Hawaii), was being cancelled. I was tan, and in good shape — I was in paradise. What in the hell happened?" He taps his happy belly.

"Life happened. You were so lucky to be in Hawaii."

"Yeah, but, also homesick. This is paradise — these moments." He raises his coffee mug in a toast-like gesture. "Do you remember about your photo's day — you know, the one where you used to be pretty?" he grins.

"Thanks. Yeah, we were gleaning, up in Paso Robles, or maybe it was Templeton."

"What's gleaning?"

"It's when you pick fruit or veggies after the harvest. We used to do it sometimes, when I was a kid. We'd pick some fruit, eat some, pick some more. It was so much fun."

Mom always loved any excuse to get out in the country to have a picnic in the hills where she grew up. One of her sisters, or maybe a cousin would reach out to a farmer the family knew to find out when the harvest was done and get permission to pick what might be left, usually grapes or walnuts. Mom would pack sandwiches, chips, lemonade and always a dessert and away we would go — about 50 miles up the road north from Santa Maria. On the trip, in said photo, I was 16 and probably at the wheel of our light-yellow Ford Fairlane, my brother and his posse of two friends in the backseat, and Mom in the front passenger control seat. She was very brave.

I haven't gleaned in years. But now I'm gleaning into my family research, to reconstruct memories, exhume new information and make well-evaluated assumptions about family tree branches and connecting them to old photos and stories.

I get lost in the photos and wonder about their lives and the actual day when each photo was taken. What were their thoughts? What did they have for breakfast? Some didn't get the chance to live a full life and age. Others, I met when they were older and never knew their younger selves.

One thing is true for all, is that time passes. Life is lived. Memories fade. And if we're lucky, we age. So, I remind myself when I walk past that photo of a happy day with my family, as my younger self, and hear in the back of my mind, "You used to be so pretty, Nana," that I'm truly grateful to be a Nana.

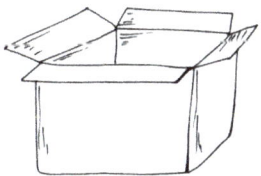

Synchronicity in Tehachapi 1987-present

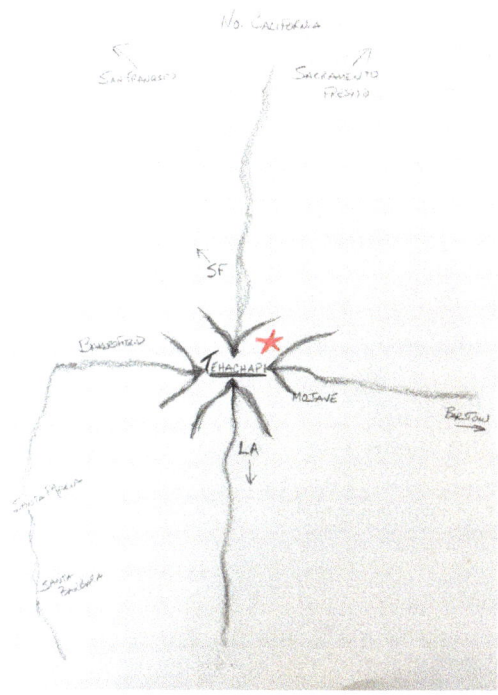

Land of Our Synchronicity, Curiosity, and Spirituality

Between somewhere and I don't care is Tehachapi. Set between Bakersfield and Mojave, of equal grey, is a picturesque community sandwiched high above California's San Joaquin Valley and high desert. Land of our synchronicity, unfolding curiosity, and uncanny spirituality.

What is it about Tehachapi? It wasn't until the coincidences accumulated that we began to take notice. What are the odds of our two families coming together in this little town even before Daniel and I were together? Was it fate or synchronicity?

It started with Daniel's life before me — a spouse, a divorced mother-in-law and her new husband. Then later, a son, his mother and a new dad, a sister and her new husband, a grandson, and now another son ended up there. On my side came — a father and stepmother, an uncle and aunt, a sister, her son and new husband. Over a 30-year period, an independent collision of lives. No central force or common thread, just a chain of migration that wove our respective family connections together.

The complex patterns and paths began when Daniel's mother-in-law remarried a local Tehachapi man. She was the first to arrive. Then Daniel's first wife came, but died a year or so later, and was buried in the local cemetery, now a place for his oldest two boys to mourn and sadly remember. His youngest son's mom married a local botanist of Tehachapi's Mourning Cloak Ranch where they made their new home.

The contribution on my side began when my uncle John and Aunt Sharon chose Tehachapi as a place to retire — a new hometown to recoup a life like it used to be. My dad and step-mom soon followed, based on his desire for a brotherly bond in elder years, and attractive real estate prices. He lived two blocks from my uncle and just an over-the-fence visit to Mourning Cloak Ranch.

Then my sister and her soon-to-be ex arrived to raise their son. She bought a home close to my dad and my uncle—just an over-the fence visit to Mourning Cloak Ranch—and remarried a Tehachapi man.

Daniel's youngest sister made her way to Tehachapi too, reconnecting with a long-lost high school attraction, who had made his home there. And now our grandson, a happy boy being raised by Daniels' sister, and our middle son who moved there, add to our many visits along the family road. They live just down the way from my sister, uncle, stepmom and an over-the-fence visit to what's now left of Mourning Cloak Ranch.

What was it about Tehachapi? Daniel and I had no history there. What are the odds of all these independent connections and migrations to this little town—a crossroads of our marriage related lives? Whether fate or synchronicity, there is meaning amidst the picturesque and grey. Family common threads now beginning to fade. The happy, the sad, deaths of those we loved, the growing away. From afar, our bond enriched, woven within history and hope. One day, Tehachapi may be just a stop between Bakersfield, Mojave, and LA.

A new old town of synchronicity, Santa Barbara, lies on the coast by the sea—a place where I may someday rather be. The town of our courthouse marriage by a spiritualist minister for fifty dollars. And the place of our common thread hospital where Daniel was born—and my dad, and then a friend, had strokes at 66, and where both died.

Beginnings, endings, and in-betweens—in this picturesque community, sandwiched between my equal hometowns, Santa Maria and LA. We continue unfolding our curiosity and uncanny spirituality, coincidentally like Tehachapi.

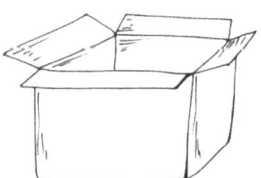

Synchronicity in England

Dodge

The decision wrecked us. Dodge, a beloved 6 ½ pound, 16-year-old Yorkshire Terrier, our grubby regal Duke of York, was given his peaceful eternal nap. The realization that our Dodge-centered life, in the time of Covid, had come to an end. The butt-wiggled tours of his castle, barks to protect from squirrel invaders, and the daily melting of our hearts, had also come to an end, as did the fluid injections, sickly days and aimless night wanderings. We miss him so.

We made the decision that when the day ultimately came, we would also have to go, travel anywhere, to distract heartache and fill the void. Our Covid-extended trip, the one that was supposed to happen two years earlier, expensive tickets about to expire, collided with the Dodge decision. A collision of emotions, another decision. Do we stay? Or do we go? Guilt invaded me. Daniel suggested we take him with us, in spirit, and extend the trip with a few days in York, England. "Let's celebrate him." Two decisions were now made.

With a heavy, yet grateful heart, we journeyed to London, Bath, Glastonbury, Bristol and then York, still with Covid-cautious face masks, perfectly packed bags and some locks of Dodge's hair. Covid changed the world, and this was another new experience, even though we have traveled a lot. We had emerged from our cocoon like a dream where the surroundings are familiar, yet different. The world was just waking up. We were changed. As the British would say, "we carried on". It was lovely, and green, people were gracious and kind.

It was clear when we got to York that Dodge was present. York is known for many things, with the Yorkshire terrier being minor compared to the heavily present medieval history and amazing countryside. Upon arrival at our hotel, "Guesthouse No. 1", across the street from the Churchill Hotel and medieval walls just a short walk away, there he was — a Yorkshire terrier statuette to greet us on the check-in desk. It reminded us of Dodge. It's the first reminder that we were in York to celebrate him.

I started to feel really rested at that point in the trip. It had been fabulous in England, not to mention getting good nights' sleep. In Dodge's last few months, he started his night wandering and whining as he tried to settle down. With "Sundowner's Syndrome", a form of dementia progressing, and some bad nights with his kidney failure, we got up numerous times, taking turns, every night. For a long time, I didn't know what a good night's sleep was and the trip was healing in many ways.

The final piece in York reminded us of our commitment. The next morning, our first morning in York, upon waking I checked my phone, a habit that followed me on the trip. The first thing that popped up on my screen was an advertisement, not my assortment of apps, or any messages. It was the face of a Yorkie, and ad for one who needed a home! "Dolly" an 8-year-old rescue. She was precious and her personality sounded just like Dodge with his little peculiarities. Was Dodge trying to tell us he was here? We got Dodge when he was 8 years old too. The universe was pulling at my heartstrings and need for comfort. And it was working. We were not coming home with Dolly, but with a reminder of Dodge's love and sweet soul.

We kept an eye out for the perfect location to do our ceremony, our little Dodge memorial. We zeroed in on the

Museum Gardens, a pretty garden we spotted on the free walking tour. It was the location of St Mary's Abbey (built in 1088), one of the many we saw on this trip, destroyed in 1539 by England's most famous menace, King Henry VIII. Ruins of a Roman wall, one that Dodge would surely pee on during a walk, would be the place. We could sit on the grass dotted with flowers growing—contemplate and say a few words to our Duke of York, Prince of Sherman Oaks, King of our castle. Our corny celebration, complete with a Whitney Houston song, "I Will Always Love You", playing from Daniel's iPhone was moving—at least to us. His little lock of hair and a picture on my iPhone, nestled between yellow and pink blooms capped our tribute. We had completed our mission. Dodge would have been pleased, and of course would have sealed it with a pee on his lovely little flowers, at the wall in the Museum Gardens in York, England.

Oddly, there were very few references to the beloved Yorkshire Terrier in York. But Daniel had learned that one pub carried a Yorkshire Terrier beer. He had to find it. A drink and toast to Dodge seemed like a good way to say goodbye to York and our celebration. We found the pub! And while we were encouraged to buy a better option (the Yorkshire Terrier beer was not a big seller or that good) but we had to do it. We made a toast and declared the trip, Dodge, and his farewell memorial so very good.

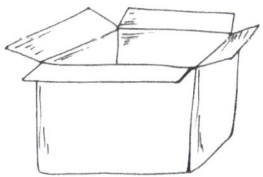

That of a Stepparent

Broken and Blended

After a rough night, my stepson reluctantly acquiesced to another try in detox and rehab. Now scooped up in an Uber, one more time, we are hopeful he won't bolt, before he even arrives. We have been down this rocky road before, but this time feels different — more dire. My husband and I recap the previous 24 hours and so many attempts prior — the usual universal Why? The addiction, the revolving door, and insanity — and what can we do differently?

Being a stepparent is a blessing and a curse. Blessed to have a chance to be a part of deserving kids' lives and a curse knowing you'll always be a reminder of the parent they wish was still there. It's just the way it is.

In my broken and blended family, many melded units, kids, and replacement parents provide opportunities to create a happy union, or sometimes just survive. Earnest and resilient souls trying to make it work, but we're all scarred. Each time, we hope we can do it better, on a mapless, sometimes thankless path. A crooked journey of silent pain, time-earned joy, and love.

It's just the way it is.

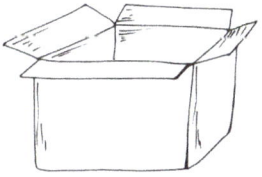

The Oak Tree

The Oak Tree

I like to call it my old oak tree, having grown it from a seedling I carefully brought home from my grandparents' ranch one childhood summer. Planted with a ring of "Hen and Chicken" succulents around its fragile twig of a trunk, I watched it mature year after year, visit home after visit home. But it's still a youngster in the life of an oak tree, not even middle-aged after over fifty expanding rings hidden inside it's huggable trunk. Maybe it watched over me too. I'd like to think so.

I cried the day I had to say a final goodbye. One last embrace. Our dog also left a gift—his mark of protection and love.

The Oak Tree with Dodge's Last Gift

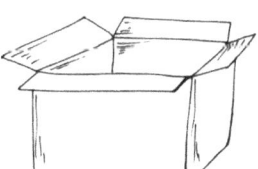

Message from Mary– Is This You?

It's nearing midnight, on an ordinary Thursday in May. May 9th to be specific. I'm night-light blurry-eyed, after making a deep dive in this small box of old black and white snapshots, probably another 200 images from my grandmother's younger years. I should be looking for a couple of other photos, on the Greenelsh and O'Neil sides of my tree that I'm convinced family ghosts have hidden, just to mess with me. Though I always seem to be drawn to the Rasgorsheks, my grandmother's young musical flirty days in the 1920s. Pulling my magnifying glass into a miniature time travel experience, my imagination flies. But weary now, I drift off to sleep.

Sleep's not happening for long. There's a photo of my grandmother posing with her saxophone, and others of friends or family with a ukulele, clarinet, or fiddle on my mind. Fun was being had and I'm right there. I noticed Edwin's name on

My Grandmother Ethelyn with Her Saxophone

one fabulous photo. Is this the same Edwin, my grandmother's cousin? Is he a musician too? I know I'm heading down a rabbit hole, but my curiosity won't let me sleep until I just do a quick peek in.

I allow only one focused look into the ancestry website family tree—Edwin Ottesen. Is there any info, something I haven't seen before? Some connection to grandma's musical past? No. Go to bed. But I see something after I leave Edwin's profile. Something big. I know I must look at this new random hint staring, maybe glaring right at me.

Could this be Mary? A new piece if information has popped up, seemingly out of the ether for my elusive great-great-grandmother, Mary Kasparak Rasgorshek. A gravesite! And an acutal death date! A confirmation of her life. Her mystery might finally

Edwin (r) and a Friend (l)

be solved. After an exhaustive search to find, and turn over every stone, she may have found me!

A moment of uncertainty causes me to pause. Shall I wake my husband to exhume this exciting discovery together, even if past midnight? Despite a desire to grasp one more piece of the family puzzle, my imaginary narrative may be shaken. Part of me wants to keep the mystery alive. I'm attached to the unknown and the freedom of my inner storytelling, perhaps creating a more captivating tale. A disappearance. A hand in her husband's unfortunate death? But it's nagging at me. Her invitation, or demand is much too strong.

What I learn from her is simple, sad, and unfortunately more common for the time. Mary survived the loss of her infant boy in 1883. She had another baby in May 1887. However, on May 10, 1887 my great-great-grandmother died of Consumption (Tuberculosis) at 32. She was buried May 11th. No time for planning a goodbye or headstone. The baby girl was also named Mary. John, Mary's husband of 14 years, saddled with children and grief remarried that December.

I whisper what I've discovered to my sleepy husband. It may take me awhile, now the wee hours of Friday, coincidently May 10th.

Name	Mary Rasgorshek
Maiden Name	Kasparek
Gender	Female
Birth Date	Jul 1854
Birth Place	Czech Republic
Death Date	10 May 1887
Death Place	Omaha, Douglas County, Nebraska, United States of America
Cemetery	Prospect Hill Cemetery
Burial or Cremation Place	Omaha, Douglas County, Nebraska, United States of America
Has Bio?	Y
Spouse	John Rasgorshek

Cemetery Record

Recipes, Rocks, Scents, and Stash

Greenelsh Cookies

A Grandma's Recipe Box

The Recipe Drawer

Signature Scent

Mom's Purse and Grandma's Knitting

A Family Thing

The Quiet Rocks

Bowl of Rocks

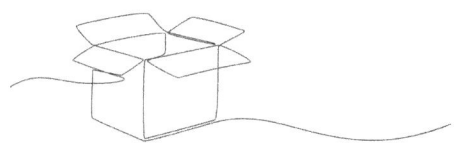

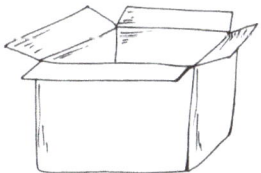

Greenelsh Cookies

Greenelsh Cookies

In the box of Grandma's photo albums and other pictures, I find "The Greenelsh Cookie" recipe on a well-used yellowed piece of note paper, with sprinkled brown stains and penciled handwriting.

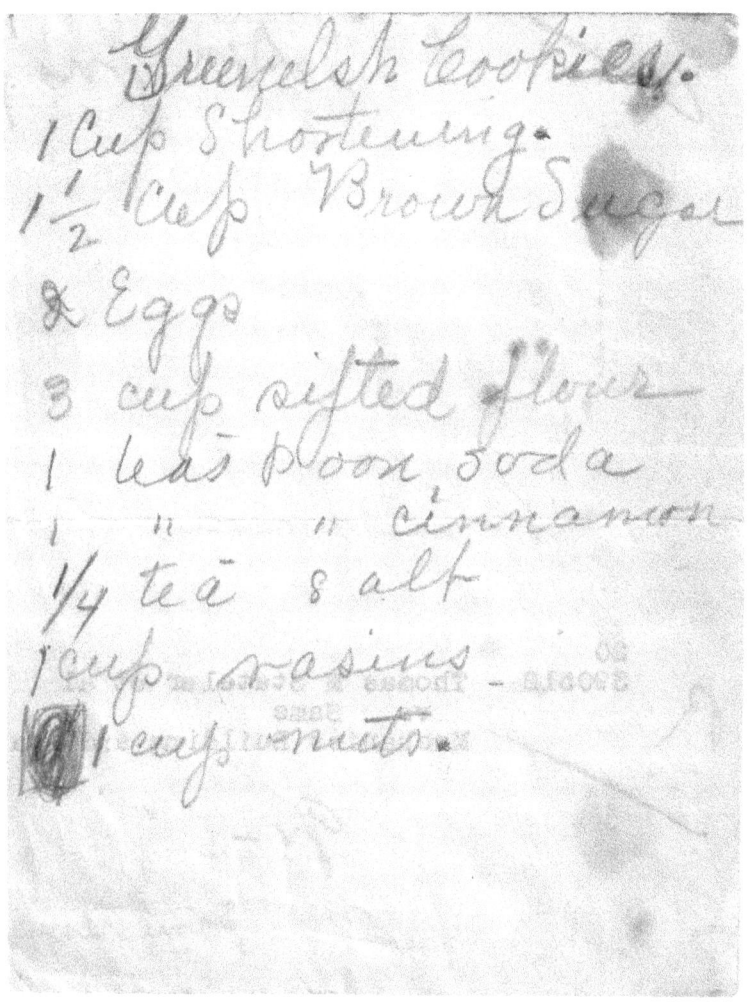

Greenelsh Cookie Recipe

It's lumped together with my great-grandfather's mechanics pass, a picture ID he used to access the jail where he worked, encased in plastic with a cigarette burn on the back. It was likely issued when he was a sheet metal worker in his earlier days in Los Angeles, when the Rasgorsheks lived in Boyle Heights.

Mechanics Pass

Was this Greenelsh recipe a well-known family cookie or just a no-name everyday cookie, passed down or made up on the Greenelsh side? Who knows if it's any good, but I'll give it a try.

I'm assuming the recipe came from great-grandma Greenelsh (Winifred). Where did she get it? Will it be a joyless batch of sweets, like her? Or did she pour her love into each attempt—her way of spreading some repressed happiness? I'll never know, but they tasted good, at least to me.

As with a lot of family recipes, I groan at the amount of shortening used. I used ½ c shortening and ½ c butter. I assumed this was a drop cookie and made each with a teaspoon. And I had to guess the oven temperature and time, so I set the oven at 350 degrees and baked for approximately 12 minutes. The recipe made about 4 dozen small cookies.

They were rustic, simple, and quite sweet. Will I make them again? Maybe, if I want to celebrate a Greenelsh tradition. It might be fun to try to enhance, modernize, and make a new and better Greenelsh family cookie.

I was not aware of any great cooking coming out of my dad's side of the family—either the Greenelsh or Rasgorshek branch. But my aunt May was known for her sugar cookies. I have fond memories of visiting her and Uncle Perry in Morro Bay, one of the better dreaded Sunday family drives. The stop included warm, just baked, brown sugar cookies served with a welcoming smile and maybe a recitation of a cute little poem Aunt May wrote, seemingly just before we arrived.

Other than Grandma's pickle recipe, there isn't a collection of cherished dishes we made for any holiday or special traditions. The classic Sunday dinner at my grandparents was an ordinary well-cooked pot roast with plain potatoes and boiled green beans, accompanied with a Jell-O salad, topped with a dab of mayonnaise. A dessert made from some new recipe clipped from a magazine or back of a box, and a good dose of family tension capped off the meal. Always predictable, and to me, it tasted good. But Grandma always found fault in something—the meat was tough, beans were overcooked (boiled to death), or the dessert didn't turn out as expected. But her sweet pickle recipe was always a hit!

Sweet Pickles

1 Jar (48 oz) dill (plain dill) pickles
Drain & slice, rinse in
water & drain well

Mix:
2 2/3 C sugar
3/4 C vinegar
(Don't mix spices in until sugar & vinegar)
2 T pickling spices.
(Put spice in thin cloth sack
& tie in ball) Your Mom
will know what I
mean. The spice is
what goes in the cloth.

(over)

Empty sliced pickles
in colander & drain well
Put sugar & vinegar in
kettle – heat & stir until
sugar is dissolved thoroughly.
Do not boil – let cool.

Put half pickles in dill
pickle jar. Then bag of
spices then rest of pickle
slices on top. Pour
cooled sugar mixture over
all. Re seal.

Refrigerate 10 days.
before. using. Leave
bag of spices in jar.
until all gone. (Hope I made myself clear)

Sweet Pickle Recipe

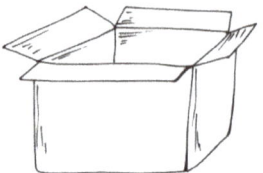

A Grandma's Recipe Box

The Recipe Box

In my mom's private stash of personal memorabilia was an old wooden recipe box—her mom Lulu's well-worn and no doubt well-loved collection. Lulu was a farmer's wife and the stories I heard growing up were through my mom's gilded-tastebud memories. Mom loved food and cooking, and much of life on her side of the family circled around the table, where stories were shared, plans were made, and traditions were celebrated. Her mom made everything from scratch and fed a cluster of farmhands daily. She plucked chickens, hauled in ice and made do with what she had. Whatever the circumstances, she always made it feel like there was an abundance of food. This side of the family was known for good cooking—a mid-west approach to hearty simple cuisine with local California produce.

The box of old index cards quickly made me realize why sweets and baked goods were popular in my family. Other than the recipe for brining 100 lbs. of pork, everything was cakes,

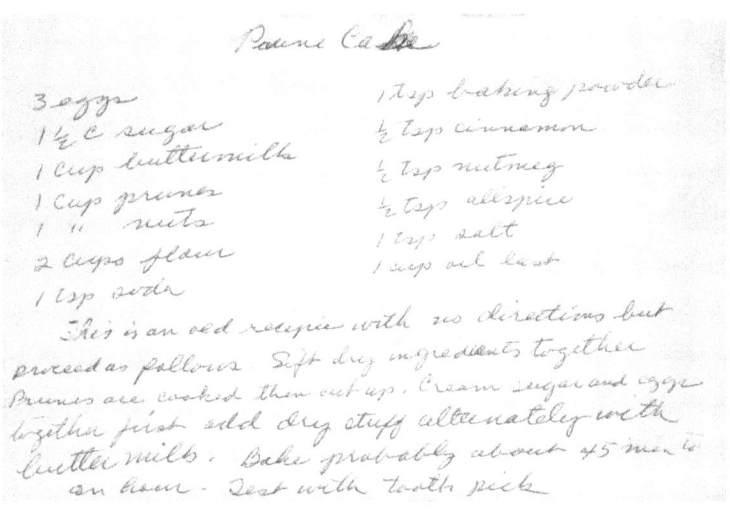

Prune Cake Recipe

puddings, and cookies. I also realized these were probably the only type of recipes that needed to be documented. Much of the other everyday cooking used what was around and was likely prepared from memory — roasted meat or game, fried or stewed chicken, boiled vegetables, sliced fruit, or the pouring of heavy cream on something, maybe anything. Common custards and bread puddings were probably known by heart, but a special occasion Devil's Food or Spice Cake not.

Mom baked frequently for a regular supply of homemade goodies, and for important events including her ultimate reward for good report cards, an excuse to make her beloved chocolate eclairs. But Mom was most known for her pies, especially the delicate flaky shortening-laden crust one, I can't seem to replicate. My favorite was apricot, with the sweet ripe fruit we'd pick from our tree in the backyard. I relish those memories of canning fruit and making jam every summer.

Mom would make two of her mom's cakes from time to time — her favorites were Applesauce or Prune Cake. I hunt for them in the wooden box to see if I can find the original source of the old timey recipes. I find ones using sour cream, mincemeat, and several cakes with prunes. Sponge cake was popular as was Cream Cake, Plain Loaf Cake or one just named Cookies.

Tucked in the front was a folded piece of letter tablet paper with notes. I read it several times and then knew exactly what it was. My mom had taken her mom's recipe box to a clairvoyant in 1997. She was interested in psychic phenomena, so this wasn't something strange Mom would do. Who knows how much the psychic really knew or saw during the time of the reading. Maybe a bit obvious, but also interesting, the psychic identified the item as something old and informative. She picked up a vision of sagebrush, tumbleweeds, dry, barren, and of hard times. And it carried a lot of love and sentimentality to the current owner. It still does.

Note from Clairvoyant

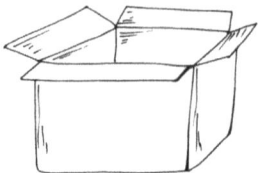

The Recipe Drawer

Like me, Mom collected memories. Tucked in shoeboxes, old shopping bags, and under beds. In my case, stored in plastic bins in my office closet amongst hundreds of old black and white photographs and other pieces of family memorabilia. One such container, bright blue with a mismatched lid, holds contents of Mom's cherished recipe drawer.

Just before leaving her empty house, emotionally done, I remembered the always-there and almost-forgotten kitchen drawer—the third down in a vertical row of four drawers—one for dish towels, one for plastic containers, the infamous junk drawer and the collection of recipes. Odds and ends, memories and possible mysteries, in a jumbled paper mess. I dumped it over into a random container—and closed the door.

At the time, I couldn't part with, sort, or process it. Like Mom, I am attached to what lurks in the assortment of recipes and who knows what got thrown into the mix. It's tucked away in my organized office closet, upside down contents ready to be excavated.

Taking a moment, sitting on my muted, blue silk meditation cushion in my office-yoga-guestroom, popcorn, and green tea within reach, I focus on my mission. Her recipes tell a story, a snapshot of her life of food, family, and history. On the surface, a trash-worthy bin. I start by sorting and organizing the mess. I do that well.

The first discovery of the fact-finding mission is a sad truth—half of the bin is my junk. I'd like to blame my husband as he's one to put things away where they don't belong, but this was probably my doing—some old work files and recipes I collected. Let's face it, Mom did not print out online recipes at work, read *Bon Appetit*, or desire Kale Mashed Potatoes.

The line is grey, as my recipe hoarding habit merges into Mom's collection in the bottom half of the bin. Though it's hard to tell if the booklets of Dear Abby's favorite recipes were hers, or something she gifted me. Over the years, she would send me clippings of recipes cut from the local paper or *Reader's Digest*, or ones she would write down from a cooking demo on an afternoon talk show. Something she thought I'd like or might help when juggling quick dinner ideas after working long hours. Her handwriting noticeably changing as she got older, her motherly suggestions still speak to me.

Finally, I get to her recipes. Clearly an older well-worn collection amassed over 50 years. Magazine tear-outs, more yellowed recipes dated with names like Chicken Almond Supreme or Peach Pie Surprise. Clippings from backs of 1960s packaged food (she loved her Cool Whip!), newspapers and recipes she picked up at the local county fair or on vacations. Organized in little piles, I sort. It seems endless, especially after I found the surplus stashed in another bin. How many recipes involving Campbell's soup or instant pudding can there be?

My mother, like many mothers in the 1960s, had just a few cookbooks — *Betty Crocker*, the kitchen staple for most cooking, now frayed with stains and crusted-batter spots on pages of those cookies and cakes she made so many times. She sent away for booklets advertised on TV or in magazines: Joys of Jello, Omelets by Candlelight for Two, or The Man in the Kitchen Recipes, a few of my favorites! Then there's the pile of hand-written recipes, many on little decorated recipe cards that were traded amongst family and friends. Or, on napkins, the back of receipts, or whatever was available to capture the prized recipe of the moment. Little notes of advice accompany varying measurement and cooking details. These are the ones that were requested, shared, and loved. Aunt Millie's Feather Frosting makes several appearances.

Then there's the pile of the odd-ball recipes — Vacuum Cleaner Bars, Watergate Cake, Amish Friendship Cake, Better Than Sex Cake, Space Syrup, and Sunday School Surprise, in addition to recipes for making clay, soap or dancing bubbles.

Lastly, is the pile of non-recipes — some food related, such as instructions for napkin folding or knife skills. And her treasures, saved Mother's Day or childhood handmade Valentine's Day cards, letters I sent during college, and other little notes that were left on the kitchen counter to communicate chores or one's whereabouts—the to-and-from of her everyday life. Little tidbits that touched her heart, and mine, on my little excavation into her past, through our shared love for recipes, food and collecting memories.

Before Mom died, she told me to look for pennies—her proposed way of saying hello from the other side. Of course, there was one at the bottom of the bin! And a note to Aquarian me in a 1994 horoscope—the back of a newspaper clipped recipe for Delicious Double Layer Chocolate Pie, *Do not waffle on a matter you need to finalize. The arrangement is worthless if it isn't closed properly.* Perhaps this time, I'll finally bring closure to this mess, keep a little and dump the rest.

Thankfully, I don't have a recipe drawer. But, the cookbook collection is growing.

Signature Scent

Always there ready to greet, embrace, or hit you upon stepping into the doorway. On the other side of the threshold, it awaits to stimulate, intoxicate, or suffocate. You know what I'm talking about. That signature scent that meets you at the door. Not the popcorn just popped or perfumy candles, but a home's signature scent—layers of life's aromas. The personality baked into the walls, hovering in the air, offering up comfort, curiosity, or a laundry list of bad habits. My mother's house always had a hint of something baked, except for a couple of years when she let the neighborhood cats roam in the house. The fond and familiar aromas (cats aside) aways brought me back home the minute I walked into the door. At my grandparents, a combination of mothballs and pot roast. At the neighbor's, homemade kimchi. In my hometown, fog, sugar beets and BBQ hung in the air. It connected and rejuvenated my momentary longing for the past.

When I sent my niece a birthday gift, a scarf from a trip I took to Bhutan, in her thank you, she told me it smelled like my house. I remembered that it had been packed in a bag with incense. But it made me wonder about what my house really smells like and if it means anything special to her. I know my home has a scented story to tell too. Hopefully, through my doorway, it's one of harmony, good cooking — and reasonably clean.

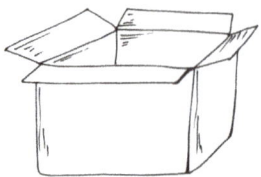

Mom's Purse and Grandma's Knitting

Mom's Purse and Grandma's Knitting

We all selected some remnants of Mom's 94 years in some form or another: a vase, knick-knacks or one of her paintings. She certainly had plenty of stuff for her kids and grandkids to divvy up when she died. Years of memories tucked into her house of 54 years.

So, why did I choose a tan leather purse? The one she bought with matching shoes. It was a strange choice, very personal, and a bit creepier as the years go by. All the contents and memories intact, frozen in time: her wallet, medical appointment cards, receipts, glasses, lipstick, the key to her house, all exactly how they were on the day she died, September 24, 2016, except for the twenty-dollar bill, of course.

Maybe because the duo purchase was made during one of her last visits — lunch and a trip to the SAS shoe store, where she took a moment to treat herself and be treated, as if she still had places to go, to be and to be seen.

The purse still sits in a corner, at the bottom of my closet.

And, I have the never-worn vest my grandmother knitted, with arthritic hands and a few muttered cuss words in a few obvious stitches — the last thing she made me. Not nearly the delicate work of her earlier days. But she made it for me — every ugly inch.

It still sits in the back of a drawer.

Maybe because it's a part of her, like my mom, I can hang on to for some submerged reason or emotion. Or maybe to just keep their memories close and a tiny thread of connection.

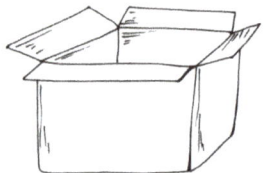

A Family Thing

Rock Collection

We like rocks!

Rocks hounded, gathered, and polished.

Polished rocks in baskets and bowls.

Bowls on living room tables and hearths.

Hearth and home, and love.

Love of our rocks.

The Quiet Rocks

Uncles

They're the ones behind the camera. The one missing from the family photo, but always there. The uncles. Stand-in dads.

Kindly in a gruff sort of way. They drive to as-needed places. With a story on the ready to tell and retell and a sometimes a questionable joke on the tip of their tongue, uncles show up—or politely stay behind and offer up a beer.

They teach how to fish, watch sports, or appreciate a barber-shop quartet or jazz. They help paint and fix things—and may have a magic trick or history lesson up their sleeve.

Perhaps underappreciated, uncles rock.

Uncles Rock

Bowl of Rocks

Bowl of Rocks

One might wonder why rocks matter to me. Early on, rock collecting was a thing we did as a family, whether beach-combing or scouring the countryside.

My husband spilled my bowl of rocks while transport-ing a table to a corner in our living room to make space for the Christmas tree. A grumble, then a curse followed by my "What are you doing? You spilled my bowl of rocks." To him, it's just that, rocks. He didn't realize it's my precious collection of family tradition and memories, Apache Tears we'd hold to the light and look through, or gaze at the amazingly clear quartz. The piece of red jasper that looks like a mini pot roast. "They aren't just rocks," I exclaimed, as he quickly scooped them up to avoid my offer of help.

Once we stumbled upon a Chumash Indian burial site and pilfered artifacts that should have been left: an old stone bowl, arrowheads, and bones. Mom was fascinated with Native American culture and used the items to educate her kids. So, it felt natural for my brother to take a few Indian bones to *Show and Tell* at school. His teacher was not impressed. They mysteriously disappeared one day — presumed to be the result of Dad's garage cleaning.

My Dad and Uncle set up rock polishers, a tumbling device in their garages. They would run for days and out would come a beautiful assortment we'd admire in a bowl in the middle of the coffee table. We all had bowls of rocks. I still do.

Mom's bowl of rocks was the mother ship. The original starter dough of family rock bowls. But my husband has out-done us all with what he calls a rock! A 2200 lb. black marble rock fountain he had placed in the middle of our backyard. The water runs down the sides like sparkling polish—a massive, polished rock.

A Rock!

Epilogue

The Richness of Family

Rock of Shame

Traits and Trauma

Sugarcoated

Layers

Oleander

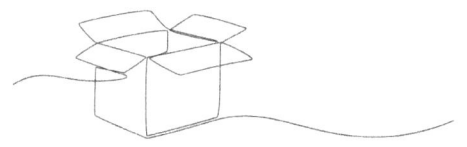

The Richness of Family

Love One Another

The richness of family —
for me broken and blended,
kept together by the need to stay together.

The traditions, celebrations, and obligations.
The wholes, halves, steps, and exes.

Respect for elders, the glue —
and belief in the value of togetherness
makes family.

Love releases hope,
softens hurt, tempers disappointment,
and nourishes young, growing lives.

Treasured memories
and acceptance of what is —
splinters again.

Rock of Shame

Rock of Shame

We may share their name, their DNA and for some, closeness to their story. Somewhere hidden under a rock of shame is that family member taking a space on a limb in the otherwise proud and revered tree. The one we don't talk about—or frankly maybe wish they didn't exist. But they do.

In our stories, they have no name. We hide them, afraid of our shame—and pain. The whole of who they were erased in our collective memory. In a desire for only perfectly-pressed laundry, we purposely forgot their innocent childhood, a productive life, and the promising light in who we once loved.

We let time pass. We carry on. We whisper. And hopefully one day we reflect, have curious wonder of why and how—and heal in the acceptance of who they became. Then quietly roll them back under the rock of shame.

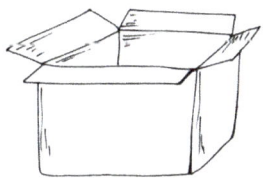

Traits and Trauma

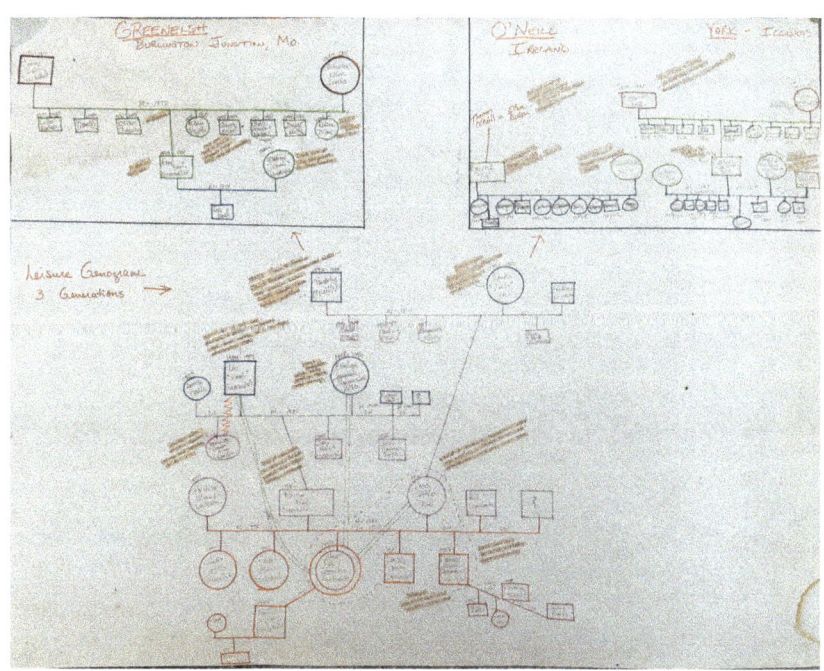

Leisure in Society Drawing – College Project

With the collection of inherited boxes, I kept an early family tree I created in college on poster board—a project in one of my favorite classes, Leisure in Society. We traced our respective genealogies to identify leisure activities passed down from generation to generation, for the purpose of learning how those activities framed family culture and societal class, and vice versa. Years later, when time allowed and my curiosity took over, I started to see how personality traits and behaviors also emerged in the tree. Clearly, I inherited genetic and cultural traits of my past, choosing to keep some traits, and shedding others. They are the bark of our family tree.

Imbedded

Epilogue

But what isn't clear or documented is how trauma imbeds itself in the fascia of the collective body. The stories and sadness not talked about. And suppressed tears absorbed in our family DNA. The shame buried in hopes of being sealed off from any possibility of perspective. There is no roadmap to follow, only evidence to uncover, and maybe some healing along the way.

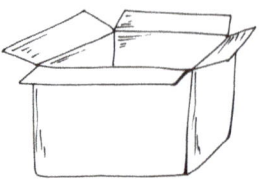

Sugarcoated

I Love You

My niece once asked me why our family never said, *I Love You*, or hugged. A true observation and valid question. And my only answer — *It's just the way we were, and sometimes still are.*

Though the act of being loving always flowed through our family, we were the family that didn't talk about our feelings or have permission to show anger. We learned to endure occasional tension, at times thick enough to cut with a knife. Family gatherings, traditions around food, our connective tissue. Good food equaled love. Conversation gracefully danced around conflict with polite manners. Make nice and when necessary, suck it up or change dancing partners.

We were also the family that always showed up, for weddings, funerals, graduations, and holidays. The exes, halves, and steps all figured it out — with the acceptance of imperfection, a dusting of humor, and gratefulness of a supportive family village, seemingly dysfunctional, but all the pieces worked in our jigsaw of a family puzzle.

A folksy handmade plaque with red and aqua letters, "Love One Another", hung over my mother's fireplace for decades. A biblical, but not necessarily religious statement in plain sight at the center of her home. Living room wisdom ready to bestow its expected of us message. A simple, yet sometimes dismissive, predetermined answer to everything. Loving one another, necessary but complicated. Read the sign, act accordingly, try to move on.

And we did — the best we stoically could, acting more than saying, accepting more than reflecting, hanging in and holding on, more than hugging.

Our family's traditional grave headstone, "In Loving Memory". Not, "Drank Too Much", or "Divorced, but Tried", or "Wish He Died in Jail". We kept a good front and sent them off knowing they were always loved, even if a few were barely tolerated. Maybe too late for hugs. But our everlasting *We Loved You*.

Layers

Dreams and History

On a hike up to the Acropolis in Athens, Greece, our tour guide imparted a fact that was hard to get my head wrapped around. There are 11 layers of civilizations in this ancient city spanning over thousands of years. Layers of dreams and history. Generation after generation. Families, life, and death. Each layer a collection of millions of moments, decisions, and choices. We as individuals all seem so insignificant, yet as time passes, something shifts because we were a part of it all — our little piece.

These boxes, I'll keep packed in layers, photos on top of Bibles, newspaper clippings on top of photo albums. One family box stacked on top of the other. Story after story, secrets remain buried. Moments, decisions, and choices left silent.

Like the rings that grow in a tree's foundational trunk, our years layer upon and within us. We age and die off. Generational personalities carve their mark in family histories, one after the other, decade after decade. Family tree branches expand, evolve and some come to a natural end. There are more layers yet to be peeled back and will continue as our DNA migrates forward. Our stories will too.

◧ Epilogue ◧

In three words, I can sum up everything I have
learned about life: it goes on.
— Robert Frost

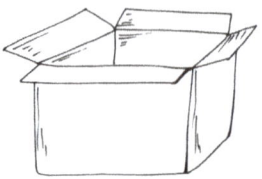

Oleander

Oleander Bush

My mother was afraid of the Oleander bush. Afraid her children might eat the leaves, consume the poison that haunted her in the occasional news story about some unfortunate family. But she never mentioned how beautiful Oleander can also be.

Our memories take us to the frightening stories and worries that get handed down. Imaginings like tattoos twisted in an Oleander haze that might devastate the family one day. But the Oleander didn't cause divorce and addiction, our customary family form of devastation, our poison.

Beauty and poison, life and death, chance and hope, envelop us all. Life is a hall of mirrors, reflecting what stories we want to believe, avoid, or twist.

The Oleander, just a choice.

Acknowledgments

A spiritual thread ran through this project and my relationship with the inherited family boxes. We became close. And by extension, I felt connected to my ancestors, as we forged along, in a time-distance relationship.

I didn't understand why I had this inner drive to dig into my family history. The boxes were talking to me, and I knew that if I didn't respond to this calling, the family history and their stories may be lost forever. The beloved photos left to be sold for 25 cents per piece at a local thrift store. Treasured memories dumped in a trash bin. It was my honor to do it and I felt a deeper purpose and thus changed, as a result.

Every time I took another dusty dive, something new would show up—a photo I'd never seen, an Aha moment with some insignificant snapshot I'd passed by in so many searches, or a renewed memory—some snippet of a story I had heard about in years past. New paths back in time were filled with new insights. What I thought were solid facts or understandings were sometimes met with a new twist, or curiosity that mysteriously popped up. Like this journey, their stories will continue to live on as I wrestle with what I know, what I think I know, and what has yet to unfold.

Synchronicity was laced through some stories. Little signs were always around, such as the fact that my husband and I have a home just a mile or so from where John and Ethel Rasgorshek had their poultry ranch on Chandler Boulevard, where my grandmother Ethelyn was raised. Or the fact that together, we have nearly 10 family members who graduated from Van Nuys High School, though we did not attend there ourselves. The ground where we live, on Ethel Avenue, was probably in the crosshairs of early family comings and goings.

When I realized my venture into merging creative writing with family research was coming together into a book project, I also learned that I had to rescan many of the old black and white photo images—a tedious endeavor. That meant finding each photo I had packed back in the boxes where I originally located them (as they had been placed decades prior) now tucked in for their long nap in the closet. Two remained elusive, as if they were colluding or trying to send a message. Work arounds were swirling. The need to find them became necessary—one more try in Box #2 that held mainly Greenelsh info and then over to one of my mom's bins.

I looked through each box and every envelope within envelopes many times—stacks of photos. I got sidetracked easily and often pulled out the magnifying glass—my looking glass into a family photo I hadn't seen before. These two caught my attention—some portion of the Greenelsh clan, early 1940s. Something happened between click one and click two. I stare and step into the laughable moment, trying to figure it out. They all look happy, even great-grandma Greenelsh (Winifred).

The Little Boy Is My Dad

But I was looking for the elusive 2"x 3" photo of Winifred, taken about 15-20 years earlier, for the *Desires Out of Reach* story. As I looked in the envelope for any remaining items to review, I happened to look down at my feet. And there it was! It had fallen out from someplace. A magical, *how can this be?* moment. Oddly enough, the other elusive photo was an easy find in another box I had also rummaged through numerous times. The stars were aligned.

The Elusive Photo

A thread of appreciation also wove through this project. I now know my roots, blood and lifelines—of who I am and where I came from—or at least better than I did going into this mission. I gained more empathy for the imperfect nature of families, and the possible healing for some, when stories and new perspectives are unearthed.

I am ever grateful for my ancestors, my relatives—all of those from the past, who were the primary focus of my writing; my siblings, David, Julia and Karen, stepmother Patty, nieces, nephews, numerous cousins, a few related exes and my aunt Gloria, who are holding up the family tree today; and to those who will carry the future torch. It's a rich tapestry I cherish.

I am also grateful for my husband Daniel, for his inspiration, input and patience while listening to my countless *Can I read you something?* requests. And for being my in-home model for a drawing class during Covid. I am also grateful for my step-children and grandchildren who enrich my life. Rounding out the circle of love, Dodge and now Kosi—the subjects of many photo shoots and belly rubs.

To my circle of girlfriends, especially those who professionally write (Dianne and Laura), you are all family too.

And lastly, I am grateful for my writing teacher Martha Fuller, for her expertise, coaching, little nudges, candid feedback and belief in my crazy quilt vision of a project. I truly appreciate her support and friendship.

APPENDIX A—YORKS AND O'NEILS GENEALOGY

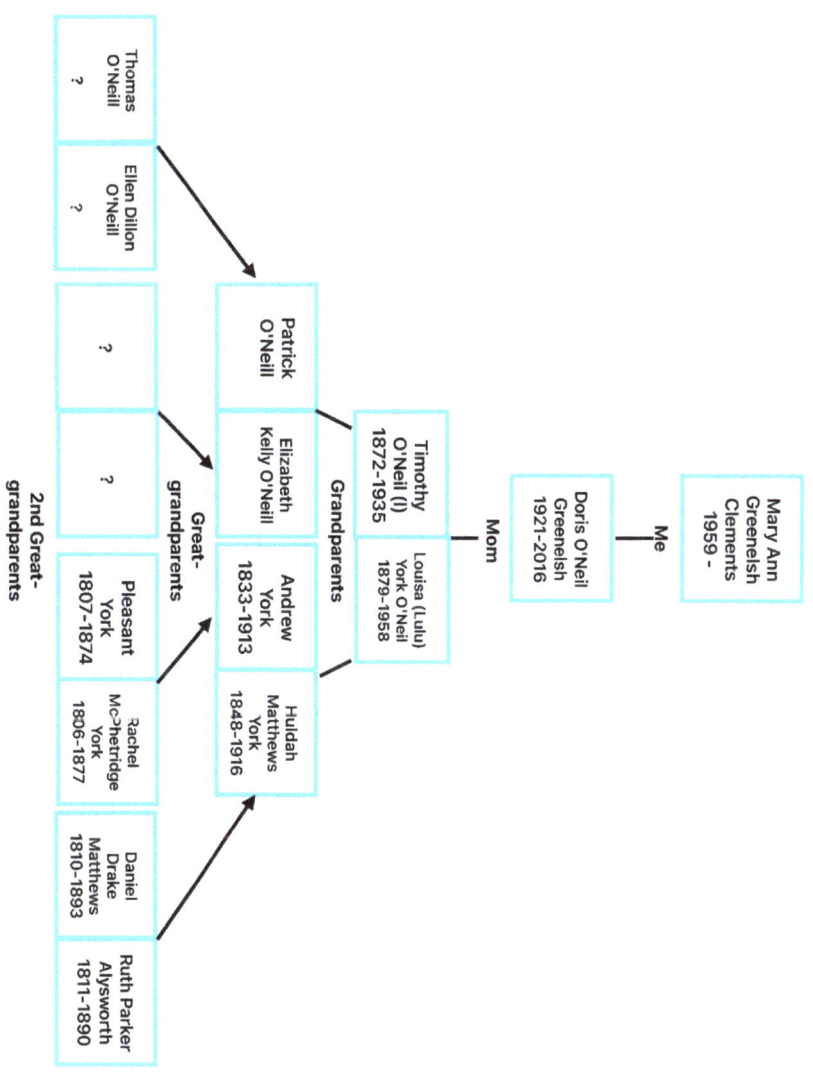

APPENDIX B— RASGORSHEKS AND GREENELSHS GENEALOGY

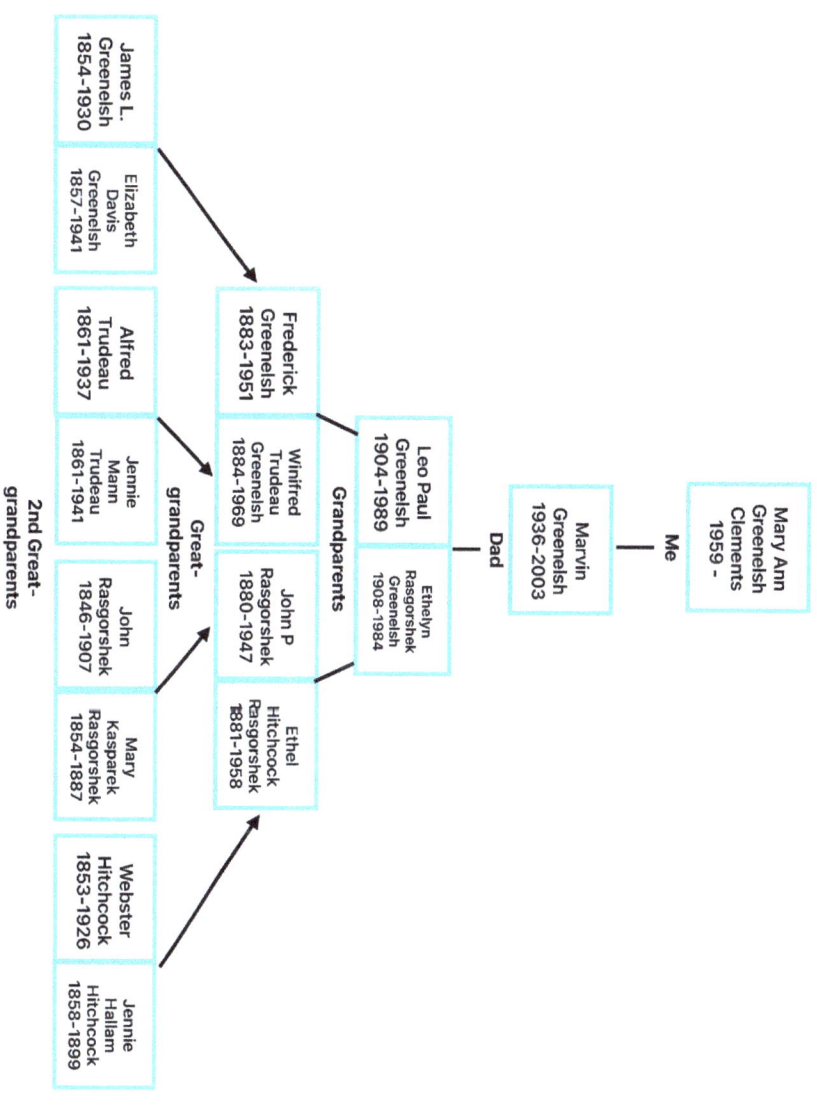

APPENDIX C—RECIPES

Greenelsh Cookies

Ingredients:

1 c shortening (if desired use ½ c shortening, ½ c butter)

1 ½ c brown sugar

2 eggs

3 c sifted flour

1 tsp baking soda

1 tsp cinnamon

¼ tsp salt

1 c raisins

1 c chopped nuts

Process:

Sift dry ingredients together.

Cream together shortening, brown sugar and eggs.

Add 1 tsp vanilla if desired.

Combine dry ingredients and wet ingredients alternating
    a little at a time.

Add raisins and nuts.

Use a teaspoon to make drop cookies, about 12-16 per cookie
    sheet.

Use parchment paper or lightly grease the cookie sheet.

Bake: 350 degrees, approximately 12 min.

Grandma's Sweet Pickles

Ingredients:

1 jar (48 oz) plain dill pickles

2 ⅔ c sugar

¾ c vinegar (we use apple cider vinegar)

2 T pickling spices (in cheesecloth sack or tied in a ball)

Process:

Drain and slice pickles. Rinse well in a colander.

Combine sugar and vinegar in a small kettle. Heat until sugar dissolves thoroughly. Do not boil. Let cool.

Put half of the sliced pickles back into the pickle jar. Add the bag of spices. Then pack the rest of the pickles on top.

Pour cooled sugar mixture over the pickles in the jar. Re-seal with the pickle jar lid.

Refrigerate for 10 days before using. Do a quick turn of the jar now and then to circulate the syrup. Keep bag of spices in the jar until pickles are gone. Keep refrigerated.

Prune Cake

Ingredients:

2 c flour

1 tsp baking soda

1 tsp baking powder

½ tsp cinnamon

½ tsp nutmeg

½ tsp allspice

1 tsp salt

3 eggs

1 ½ c sugar

1 c buttermilk

1 c chopped prunes

1 c chopped nuts

1 c oil

Process:

Sift dry ingredients together.

Cook or soak prunes in hot water so they can be chopped easily.

Cream eggs and sugar together. Add to sifted dry ingredients, alternating with buttermilk.

Add prunes, nuts and lastly the cup of oil. My mother would likely add a tsp of vanilla too.

As this is an old recipe, details are sketchy. Mom used a rectangular baking pan and usually greased and dusted with flour before adding the batter.

Probably bake at 350 degrees for 45 min to an hour. Test with toothpick.

APPENDIX D—CLAIRVOYANT NOTE

Found in My Great-grandmother's Recipe Box

The note's handwriting is not my mom's. She either went to the psychic with a friend, who took the notes, or a friend brought it to the psychic on her behalf and made notes.

The old recipe box belonged to my mom's mother, Lulu, who lived in the hills west of Templeton, then Paso Robles, on the California coast.

————

(Not looking at the front)
Immediately felt like the old view graph thing.

Pleasure, fun, enjoyment (not the right words). Informative (right word). Whatever the picture is it was/is informative.

Feels dark, not in weight, but in printing, background, not necessarily color.

I feel a lot of love when holding this, sentimentality by person who owns this now.

A place to back into time.

Heart chakra, breathe in the feelings of the time, the scent in the air, the mood of the moment. It touches the heart.

No sensation at throat chakra – just is.

3rd eye – plains, sagebrush, vastness, tumbleweeds, barren, dry – hard times (old fashioned bathing suits & the ocean).

3/26/1997 – Doris's recipe box

◘ Appendix E ◘

APPENDIX E—LIST OF ILLUSTRATIONS

BIBLIOGRAPHY

References

Greenelsh Pedersen, Olive Jean, *The Olive Branch*. 2010

Guinn A.M., J.M. *History and Biography – History of the State of California and Biographical Record of the Santa Cruz, San Benito, Monterey and San Luis Obispo Counties*. Chicago: The Chapman Publishing Co., 1903

Peasley, Helen (Auntie Hi), "Research and Writings". 1970s

Online Resources

Ancestry
http://www.ancestry.com

Newspapers
https://www.newspapers.com

ABOUT THE AUTHOR

Mary Ann Greenelsh was born and raised in the heart of her family roots on California's Central Coast. College and a desire to leave a small town brought her to Southern California, where she also had family connections. She acquired a BS degree from California State University, Northridge. In her career as a travel industry professional, she held several management positions. Her last position prior to retirement was Corporate Travel Manager with an aerospace firm. Mary Ann's interests now lie in the creative arts, family research, and of course travel. She resides in Los Angeles with her husband and a cute dog, Kosi.

This book is typeset in Book Antiqua, a Roman typeface based on letterforms of the Italian Renaissance. Display type is Spumoni LP and Cormorant Upright.

www.ingramcontent.com/pod-product-compliance
Lightning Source LLC
Chambersburg PA
CBHW051608120626
46551CB00014B/1713